Contents

Title Page
About the Book
Must Love Sand
Has Anyone Ever Popped Into Ikea?
Snatched
Tooth Fairy Trouble: How Much?
Shopaholic in Dubai
The Big-Ticket Present
To Slide or Not to Slide?
The Robot Help
The Pearl Divers
Cellmates
Travel with Kids: The Bad and the Worse
Risky Business
The Driving Lesson
Cupcakes & Heels
Acknowledgments

Marianne Makdisi

Circles in the Sand
Stories about life in the Big D

Illustrations by Renato C
Contributors: Inessa Jackson; Lucy Titheridge;
Lynn Maclean Willmoth

About the Book

Hello and welcome to my collection of short stories!

The book was born from my blog, Circles in the Sand (dubaiunveiled.com) – an often funny, true-to-life expose of daily goings-on in the Big D. I write it when the kids aren't looking, and when I'm not too distracted by living in a city full of souks, skyscrapers, shopping, sea and sand.

No topic off-limits, the blog aims to dispel the myth that all expat mothers in Dubai are gin-swilling, diamond-clad, double-kissing Jumeriah Janes who continually palm their children off on the housemaid to hunt down the latest designer handbag (*No really, we don't!*).

The book includes the best of the blog and much, much more. I hope you enjoy all the stories and posts that follow.

Must Love Sand

Fun mum needed for lifelong position in growing international company (Trailing Spouse, Inc)

Roles and skills required

Domestic engineer (fix broken toys, leaks, the Internet)

Director of child development (must be available 24/7 and responsive at 3am)

Senior buyer (why go to one supermarket, when you can go to *three* to get everything you need?)

Chef (Tesco ready-meals are a *looo-ng* way away)

Risk analyst (if another mum picks up your child, will she use a car seat?)

Fashionista (full make-up, sundress and heels by 7.15am)

Diplomat/negotiator (small warring countries are a *cinch* compared to hot, overtired siblings)

Chauffeur (long-distance/defensive driving experience on supersized highways preferable)

Creative director (how many days stuck inside in the air-con can you fill creatively?)

Home studies supervisor (how long till *you* lose the plot?)

Translator (French, Arabic, Hindi)

Event coordinator (two children, three parties, one mum)

Stylist (kids must be well turned-out, shoes clean enough that you can see design/original colours, hair combed)

Investment manager (prices of bread, fruits and fish fingers need to be monitored to avoid bankruptcy in Spinneys)

Counsellor (pick up the pieces when grandparents leave or school friends move back home)

Specific duties related to spouse

Greet within two minutes of arriving home or be accused of mood swings

Muster energy to spend evening talking coherently

Look presentable (clean clothes, make-up reapplied and definitely no elastic)

Salary

Ha! (Unless you count the coins that drop out of the dryer after a load of laundry)

Benefits

Happy, healthy children raised as global nomads. Blue skies and sunny days. Travel. Bucket-loads of love.

Has Anyone Ever Popped Into IKEA?

Disclaimer: The words below are arranged randomly; you will need to assemble the finished story yourself

"I've got a pain in my chest!" Neil twists his face into a tortuous grimace. A hand flies from the steering wheel to his throat.

    My mouth falls open – he can't be having a heart attack. Not on the road. Not turning off the highway into Festival Centre. Geez – he's just had a medical with an ECG and all sorts of tests. He's only 44, for Christ's sake.

    "I think I've got …" He coughs. Wipes his brow with the back of his hand. "… IKEA-itis."

    "Ah-ha," I say, relaxing. I shoot him a sideways glance, and lay my palm on his knee. Wearing khaki shorts, his kneecap feels bony and warm, a few coarse, black hairs curling outwards. I give it a playful squeeze, hoping to assuage my guilt. I'd sort of tricked him into coming. A casual, *"Well since we're over this side of town, we might as well pop into IKEA for those curtains."* I'd said it brightly as though I'd suggested a trip to the pub. We'd locked eyes, and he'd sucked air in between his teeth then blown it out slowly through his cheeks. Let's just say, I promised him I'd make it worth his while.

As the cheery yellow logo on the side of the gigantic blue building looms into view, I run through my list in my mind.

"Just curtains," says Neil.

"Yep," I reply.

The fib falls easily from my lips. I get away with it as Neil is distracted by the busy parking garage. We both scour the rows of SUVs, looking for the last vacant spot.

Neil eventually parks, cuts the engine and hesitates. "I could wait for you here?" He tugs at his earlobe as his features bunch up into a pleading expression. His face already looks drained. "If there's any heavy lifting involved, just text me and I'll be right there."

I know he's remembering the time we both had to suppress murderous fury as we stood in Bedroom Furniture debating which pillow covers best accented our duvet. And, if I'm honest, his gruff words at the end of that visit that IKEA is 'relationship kryptonite' are ringing in my head like a toll bell. "But this is just a quick visit," I say, persuading myself as much as him. I suggest eating first.

"Alright," he says, brightening. "Let's get this over with."

**

With the taste of gravy-covered meatballs and fluffy mash still in our mouths, we walk out into the stark, artificial light of the main concourse full of resolve. I grab an enormous yellow bag from a smiling man who looks drugged.

Neil raises his eyebrows. "You really need that?"

"Just in case," I shrug.

We agree to divide and conquer the vast Swedish budget-furniture emporium. Neil wants to check out garden furniture, while I've just remembered we need a new BILLY bookcase (*"Think how good you'll feel after putting it together, sweetie – all carpenter-y and triumphant,"* I say, looking up at him through my fringe.) Then the plan is to meet by the curtains.

Well, I take a bit longer than I meant to – but that always happens in IKEA, doesn't it? It has a way of sucking you in so that forty-five minutes later you're still lapping kitchens and office furniture. There are just so many options and ideas, so many eye-catching room layouts in pine and white with bright soft furnishings and clever storage solutions.

I could happily *live here*.

Next I start thinking I could use almost everything I see. Those cute pencils. That gadget that froths milk. That 100dhs thingamagig that hangs on the wall to keep bits and pieces in. Surely we could use a lamp, or three?

I claim a spare trolley and transfer the contents of my bag, sparing my shoulder from being wrenched from its socket.

My phone rings.

"Where are you?" says Neil. He sounds desperate. He says he knows a shortcut. He's worked out all the shortcuts in IKEA – doors that look like fire escapes; doors barricaded with trolleys, or piled high with boxes. He's been through them all, looking for the nearest exit.

He has a theory that IKEA is like modern society. You start at one end, and get funnelled through a set path, while being continually sidetracked by shiny objects that both dazzle and throw you off balance. His shortcuts are doors that say 'You don't have to tread the same route as everyone else'. There's *another way*. He's even discovered the big short-cut, the get-out-of-jail one. Wide silver doors that shout KEEP CLOSED. FIRE EXIT and lead directly to the checkouts.

"Okay, I'm coming," I promise. "No more shopping – straight to curtains."

I push through a door thinking it's the right way, only to come out in a beautiful area of kitchen organisers and the latest Tupperware. ON SALE! The sound of a child howling as his mother crams piles of kids' multi-coloured plastic plates into her bag ensures I hurry on. I'm also anxious now not to keep Neil waiting any longer.

The haberdashery section is relatively quiet compared with the bustle and haphazardly parked buggies in the rest of the store. There's just an Emirati woman buying drapes for a ten-bedroom villa, and a harassed mum with an overexcited daughter treating the store like an adventure playground.

Neil pulls out a twill-weave curtain in pigeon grey – a slated and solemn colour I saw too much of in London – and I realise we'll never agree. He shifts his weight uncomfortably from side to side while I browse as fast as I can, absorbing the feel of the textures with the pads of my fingers. Wool-blends, chiffon, cotton duck, velveteen, non-sheer silk (with 'great drapability'). We're spoilt for choice. Until it comes time to order.

Sanjay, our badge-wearing assistant, shakes his head at least four times. "No Ma'am, not in stock." "Ran out yesterday, sorry!" "Maybe in two weeks."

I begin to think they don't actually sell curtains – maybe the pretty fabrics are just decoration?

My teeth gritted, I recall the last time the staff told us the item we wanted wasn't in stock. Neil tapped the app on his phone and showed the assistant there was one left in the warehouse. We were right, we won, and I swear other couples cheered for us.

Finally, I settle on two designs they actually have material for. I give Sanjay my measurements (the windows, not mine), and point out a scribbled, spidery number on the order form that could easily have resulted in drapes sixty centimetres too short. Who knew curtain assistants could rival the handwriting of doctors in the indecipherability stakes? I'm determined they're going to get it right first time.

Sanjay taps away at his computer then hauls the rolls of fabric over to my trolley. Odd, I think. *Doesn't he need to keep the material to turn it into curtains?*

"No, Ma'am. After check out, you take it to customer services, aisle five."

Of course.

After paying, Neil pushes the trolley to a line of counters. His shoulders have slumped and he pauses for a moment to rest his elbows on the cart's handle. He looks longingly at the exit and checks his watch several times. There's nobody manning aisle five, and even I'm beginning to feel claustrophobic.

It's a funny old corner: cardboard boxes in all shapes and sizes, IKEA staff scuttling in an out of a warehouse like worker ants, customers languishing on seats. "I was lost in IKEA for three days once," I hear someone joke. "Only went in for tea lights."

To hand in our would-be-curtains for tailoring we have to take a ticket from the machine and wait for our number to flash up on the screen, like in a passport office. So we pass the time watching the vacant souls around us, the minutes crawling by like treacle from a narrow bottle neck, Neil drumming his foot on the lino … until, nearly three hours after walking into the store 'just to buy curtains', we make it out of there. Still speaking.

"But did you really *need* those heart-shaped salt-and-pepper shakers?" asks Neil as he loads up the car, shaking his head.

"Well, maybe not … but I had to buy them or I'd never be able to find them again. I could nip in and take them back quickly?"

"No, it's fine. They're great. Just what I always wanted."

Snatched

I'd just dropped my kids at school for the first day back after the Christmas holiday, and was returning (read: skipping with unabashed joy) to the car – *four* child-free hours ahead of me – when I bumped into her.

    We all know her. She's the mum who follows her young up slides, down plastic tubes and into the toilet. All mothers share her protective tendencies to varying degrees, and hover over our offspring at times, but Helicopter Mum has taken this to a new level by being *hyper-present* in her children's lives.

She's standing half-hidden behind a palm tree, sobbing into her hankie. Big fat tears and Bobbi Brown mascara streaming down her crumpled face.

My bolt for freedom screeches to a grinding halt and I stop to ask if she's alright, aware that those four *precious* hours (in which I planned to knock out several chores in double-quick time, buy a week's worth of groceries *and* get a blow-dry) are already slipping away.

"We had such a wonderful holiday," she blubs, dabbing at her puffy, red-rimmed eyes, pert chest rising and falling beneath fuchsia pink activewear. "I wasn't *ready* for term to start again." My hand goes to the strap of my handbag, and I hoist it higher onto my shoulder, unable to keep still, but feeling sorry for her nevertheless. "It was over before I knew it," she says. I give the tiniest nod.

She draws a deep, shaky breath and regales me with sniffly tales about the cookies they baked, the trip to see Santa and the Christmas stories her children wrote, while I almost start twitching with the urge to get going. The school has emptied of parents now and the bell has already rung. With registration underway, the only real noise is the low hum of continuous traffic on the twelve-lane highway I should be cruising along to start my first chore at Silicon Oasis.

Beyond her svelte, gym-toned figure, I see, in the corner of my eye, the school security guard pull out a bunch of keys. Backlit by the morning sunshine, he propels them into the air and they land in his palm with a jangle. We'll be locked in if we don't get moving, fast. I push my sunglasses onto the top of my head, steal a glance at the time on my phone and recalculate: *I'll do the big shop tomorrow. I'll be a good friend this morning.*

Helicopter Mum brightens noticeably when – to get her *off* the school grounds – I suggest a (quick) coffee. "That would be smashing," she gushes, "much better than going to the gym," and I watch as the pained look on her face turns into a wide smile. It's the death knell for that morning's to-do list, but at least it might *stop* her calling her oldest on his mobile – the world's *longest* umbilical cord – at break time.

Two hours and four lattes later, we walk out of the coffee shop. She gathers me into a hug. She smells like a posh department store and her diamond earring presses hard into my cheek. "Wonderful to see you sweetie!" she trills, gold bracelets clanging together as she drops her arms back to her side. "I feel so much better now."

SHE might feel more upbeat, but now I know, in detail, the long list of extra-curricular activities she's lined up for her offspring, a vein in my head starts throbbing as I imagine the headache she's going to give job recruiters when she demands to know why her Precious Angel has been passed over.

***

Later that morning, less than half my errands completed and my hair still falling in lank, shoulder-length curtains around my face, I prepare lunch for when my youngest gets home. The kitchen window is open, and the smell of cut-grass wafts in. The gardeners are mowing, pushing a rusty, old-looking piece of machinery up and down the lawn.

When the drone of the motor stops, silence rushes in, broken only by birdsong and a distant bark from a neighbour's dog. The sky is cloudless and blue, and the bougainvillea against the back wall almost looks too brilliant to be real, climbing frothily towards the sun in a bloom of pink, orange and white.

I push my fringe off my forehead and keep stirring the cheese sauce, checking it's the right consistency, not too runny, not congealed. The sauce is at a make-or-break stage, and I'm enjoying the last moments of peace before my boisterous boys return from school.

It's not that I didn't enjoy their school holidays – the way they stampeded around, crashing and yelling and fighting for the past week. It's just that, after a prolonged period of noise – so loud and jarring it even rattled the pans on the shelf in the kitchen – I long for quiet, and some space to think.

Glancing at the clock, I see it's nearly time to leave. The little ones finish ridiculously early, and if I don't go in the next five minutes, I'll be late. Wiping my hands down my jeans, I quickly clean up the kitchen, grab my handbag and fly out the door. The car's locking system opens with a click and I climb in. My phone rings as I'm rummaging around for my sunglasses.

It's *her*, Helicopter Mum, and she's so breathy with distress, I think it's a prankster at first.

"My car won't start," she gasps. "I can't get to school."

"Don't worry," I say. "I'll bring Trixie home, no problem at all."

But it *is* a problem, because Trixie has never been in anyone else's car before. It's never been necessary, because Helicopter Mum is always *there*. She's attended every single sing-along, accompanied all the school trips and never missed a single pick-up. From the day her children were born, she's lovebombed them into submission.

"I'll bring her straight back," I promise, and with no other option, she agrees.

***

I tune in and out of the noise coming from the back of the car. Trixie and my second-born, Max, are practically doing hightails in their car seats they're so excited to be coming home together.

I'd always thought daughters were quieter than sons. Not Trixie. She's a talkative, kooky-looking girl with green, slanted eyes. But that hair! It loops in strawberry-blonde ringlets around her porcelain face, giving her features a colourful border and creating a thick bundle of curls. She looks incredibly sweet, until she's crossed, and then her bottom lip protrudes like a ledge, her brows snap together and she takes on the air of a wronged princess.

"Mummy says we're going to Oman this weekend," she announces with a Tigger-like bounce. "Will you come Max?" she demands loudly. In the rear mirror, I see her staring at my son from under her lashes. "We're going business class," she says, injecting as much 'wow' factor into her brag as possible.

A jab in my back startles me. She's kicked the back of my seat in excitement.

"Hey," I respond. "No kicking." A minute passes. Another stab, this time harder.

Frowning, I give both passengers another warning, and glance in the mirror again when the kids go quiet. A red-top taxi fills the mirror, so close I can make out the driver's features. He's practically riding my bumper, his plate number clearly readable backwards. I let out a small, exasperated sigh. *Doesn't anyone in this city know how to drive safely?*

I turn my eyes back to the road and concentrate on the tarmac ahead, seeing, in my peripheral vision, the familiar expanse of desert streak by. Camels, sand dunes and towering, industrial-sized electricity pylons flash past. And then we're passing the far edge of a compound of newly built villas – Arabian-style, mustard yellow homes, with tall, arched windows, balconies and decorative turrets. Each one an identikit copy of the next. A gigantic billboard rises up from the scrubby, dust-filled landscape; it always makes me laugh. "BUY A HOME. GET A CAR," it says in a bold, shout-out-loud font. "GUARANTEED!"

"Mum," says Max, bringing my mind back into the car with a jolt.

"Yes."

"There's a crazy lady waving at us."

"Where?" I ask, putting my foot on the brake as the traffic light ahead flashes orange.

"In the taxi, behind us."

I bring the car to a halt at the traffic signal and crane my head round to look out the rear window. I'd recognise that face anywhere; it's a face that in six years hasn't got any older. Eyes a little too wide-awake, forehead free of lines, eyebrows plucked into thin curves. Helicopter Mum is sitting in the back of the taxi, leaning forwards through the gap between the seats, gesticulating wildly. *What on earth is she doing?*

I lift my hand to give a slow wave as she clamps her phone to her ear. Mine rings from inside my handbag. I tell the children it's Trixie's mum, not a crazy lady (although of that, I'm not convinced), and then pull my phone out. The ringing stops. There are seven missed calls and four text messages. Swallowing hard, I quickly scan the screen:

> "Don't worry about the pick-up, coming to school in a taxi!"
>
> "On my way – be there in 5"
>
> "Everything ok?"
>
> "Why r u not answering? <worried face emoticon>"

Judging by the anxious – no, frightened – look on Helicopter Mum's mask-tight face, I haven't actually been terribly helpful at all. She's got me on her radar. I've *kidnapped* her darling, bubble-wrapped Trixie. Should I pull to the side and hand her daughter over? I wonder.

Trixie snaps her head away from the rear window. Jutting her chin, she flops back into the seat like a marionette with its strings cut. Our gazes lock and I notice steely flecks of grey in her irises. Her bottom lip shoots out as she folds her tiny arms across her chest.

"Do you want to ride with your mummy?" I ask.

"No," she replies, giving a single, terse shake of her head, her face carved from stone. "I want to go home with Max," she says, just as the light turns green. I make a snap decision.

When we get back to the Helicopter family's house, I'll ask if Trixie would like to come home with us for a play on a regular basis. Perhaps even suggest a few activities Helicopter Mum might like to try to take her mind off parenting for a while, like the Wednesday morning mums' paddleboarding lesson round the Burj al-Arab and our monthly games of Bunco.

This little bit of separation from Trixie will do them both good, I decide and I accelerate across the junction, a smile tugging at my lips and my foot tapping the pedal just a tiny bit harder than it might have done otherwise.

Tooth Fairy Trouble: How Much?

By Lynn Maclean Willmoth

"How much did you get?" Even children newly informed about the Tooth Fairy are already in no doubt about the true relevance of her visit.

Although few and far between, opportunities to get away from it all for a day or two pop up for most families. Time being of the essence, I started to consider a 'staycation' – a holiday at home – and what better place than the Atlantis?

Built on The Palm – land reclaimed from the sea and shaped into a colossal palm tree – guests not only stay in the most beautiful rooms and play around elegant pools and beach huts, they can also get up close and personal with dolphins. To top it all, The Atlantis hosts Aquaventure, a magnificent aquatic theme park filled with so many different types of water slides and play areas it's hard to cover them all in one day.

Sounds fabulous, doesn't it? *Of course*, there's something for everyone; *of course*, we all want to go; *but of course*, once a few enquiries have been made the shout comes up as "...HOW MUCH?" However, after more than four years in Dubai, eventually along came the opportunity to justify a visit – and how can we possibly not go *just once?*

The room was indeed splendid and thanks to some clever sliding door/wall trickery the children could even watch TV in the bath. The food was top class; again, "...*how much...?*" we cried weakly as we melted into some of the best Italian food we have ever had.

The highpoint, however, was indeed Aquaventure; two whole days of sliding and splashing, screaming and laughing, floating and gliding, at the end of which the children (and me!) crawled back to our room to sit, motionless, in the bath and roll straight into bed without a single protest.

This was especially so for one little boy, who, after weeks of wobbling, finally lost another tooth during our stay. The minor incident of only realising it was gone over a sumptuous breakfast resulted in my husband making a break-neck dash to get back to the room before housekeeping to pluck this little tooth from between the sheets. Because of course, *wherever* you are, the Tooth Fairy will *always* come…. (*phew!*)

"Will the Tooth Fairy definitely know we're at the Atlantis?" asked my tired son that night, his head and body folding up into the sheets like an envelope. "Of course darling," I crooned, "She knows *exactly* where you are," and with that he fell fast asleep.

I was quick to follow; falling face down into those pristine white sheets, only vaguely aware that my husband was leaving to go downstairs to meet up with some friends we'd bumped into that day.

On returning to our room, he had the wherewithal to remember to remove the precious tooth and pop a note down in its place. In the UAE, even small amounts are represented in note form, 5dhs (approximately 85p or $1.35) being the smallest.

But *where* could he find this 'change'? He didn't appear to be carrying any himself. Aren't I *always* the person to be relied upon to supply just the very small amount he always seems to be without? Aren't I always the one with that extra dirham required for the parking meter? After fumbling around for my bag in a very dark… (boy, those blackout curtains were *good!*)… and did I say, *glorious*, room, my husband finds my purse and wrestles a note from within.

Morning arrives, and the children wake up first, of course. As my husband and I are dragging ourselves into consciousness, the squeals of delight start. I'm instantaneously horrified that I forgot all about Tooth Fairy Duty and equally grateful that my husband had not.

"Mummy! Daddy!" shouts our son. "The Tooth Fairy! She *found* me!"

We manage all the right noises as we struggle to remain horizontal with two excited children now bouncing up and down on our bed.

"How *much* did you get?" asks his sister.

"TWO HUNDRED DIRHAMS!!!!!!" he exclaims! Both of us bolt upright in bed, "HOW MUCH…?"

We were powerless. Utterly powerless, just about managing, "Yes darling, THAT.IS.A.LOT of money. Yes, it *must* have been because she was The Atlantis Tooth Fairy. And …er, yes…she's *very* generous."

The incident left us with two problems: How to *not* give a small boy nearly £34/$55 for one tooth; but worse, *how* to keep him quiet? We did manage to prise the precious note out of his clutches – *with* the promise of an ice cream. But great were my blushes at the school gate as mothers cast those *oh-so* critical looks.

Shopaholic in Dubai

By Lucy Titheridge and Marianne Makdisi

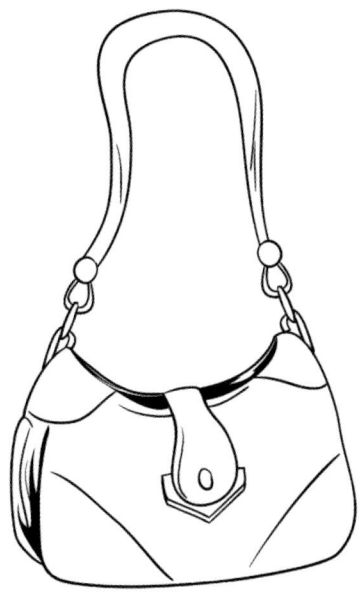

Daniella

Daniella stared at her phone, willing it to ring. Where the hell had Katie got to? She called her mobile for the seventh time, and left another message, even more desperate than the last. *"For God's sake, call me – please."* Then she tapped out a text, sent it and stabbed 999.

    A male voice answered almost immediately.
    "Which service do you require?"
    "Police," replied Daniella, breathlessly.
    Another man came on the line and said, "Can I help you?"
    "I want to report a missing person," blurted out Daniella. "My friend's on holiday here, and she hasn't come home. She's

been gone for hours – since midday." A quick glance at her watch confirmed that it was almost eight pm. "I can't get hold of her. This is just really unlike her. She should have got back ages ago."

Daniella's whole body froze as she spoke her worst fears aloud. "I'm scared she's been abducted. She went to Karama … to buy a handbag," she said in a quieter voice, "and promised she'd come straight back. We had plans–"

"I'll just put you through to the right department," interrupted the man on the other end. A lengthy silence followed, then came a click and the sound of a third, lower voice. Daniella took a deep breath and started again.

"What's your friend's name ma'am?" asked the police officer.

"Katie. Katie Rawlins."

"Are you sure she isn't just smoking the hookah somewhere?"

Infuriated by his dismissive tone, Daniella shot back, "I'm quite sure – she would have told me. She'd have sent a message. I think she might have got in a car with one of the handbag sellers."

Even as she said it, she was blaming herself. If only she'd gone with Katie, then she wouldn't be sitting here panicking on a Thursday night, imagining that her childhood best friend had been kidnapped, or worse, murdered by a bearded handbag salesman. Guilt prickled her conscience like ants crawling under her skin.

The officer asked her to stay on the line while he found the right form and she heard him rummaging around, rifling through papers, lazily shuffling sheets. Why wasn't he more concerned? She picked at the arm of the chair and smelt the toast she'd burnt after calling the restaurant to cancel their dinner reservation.

Walking over to the window of her twentieth-floor flat, she gazed out at nighttime in Dubai. A carpet of lights twinkled across the city. Katie was out there, somewhere. A new thought dropped into her head like a stone into water. Maybe she'd been in a car crash. *Perhaps I should have called the hospitals first.* Her own reflection stared back at her, her lips clenched thin and her hair messy.

"I'll just get some details from you," said the police officer, coming back on the line, sounding tired and a little bored, "then we'll take it from there."

***

Daniella took a taxi to Karama, where the police officer had agreed to meet her. She sat back, pinned to her seat, as the taxi diver veered onto the highway and slalomed over to the fastest lane in seconds. Prayer beads jangled and the bleeper went off as he accelerated through the speed limit. The boy racer in him wasn't going to let the busy end-of-the-week traffic get in his way. "Slow *down!*" she wanted to say, but didn't. At least she'd get to Karama in no time, probably before the police.

"Could you turn the AC up," she said instead. His fingers fiddled around with an air vent in the back, and she thanked him, willing him to notice the chorus of red brake lights ahead. The traffic was slowing. Muscles twitched in her leg as she repressed the urge to slam her foot down on an imaginary brake pedal. She lurched forwards as they lost speed suddenly, and only released her grip on the seatbelt when they joined the end of the traffic jam, from there on proceeding forwards in a stop-start fashion.

As she stared out the window at the brightly lit skyscrapers and flashing neon signs, her mind went over the events of the day before. Katie's visit had been flying by – sunbathing, the beach, the pool. Daniella had some time off work and was enjoying playing tourist rather than working eleven-hour days in Internet City. Yesterday, they'd been on a mission, to buy handbags. It had been a while since she'd last visited Karama's fake handbag shops, and when they got there, she'd been surprised to find that the once-bustling area was now devoid of the traditional big-name brands. Police raids had seized much of the stock, and the infamous back rooms and attics were now sealed off.

They'd been approached by a dark-haired man who'd asked if they wanted copy bags. "We have Jimmy Choo, Mulberry, we give you good price," he said.

Daniella and Katie had glanced at each other, nodded their agreement and then followed him down an alley, up another one, through the winding streets until they reached a doorway. There he led them up some stairs to a thick bolted door, which he knocked twice on and waited. They heard the scraping of bolts being drawn back, then the door opened and they were ushered into a room that was wall-to-wall full of bags – hundreds of them, all shapes, sizes, colours and makes. Another furtive salesman thrust an iPad under their noses showing photos of their hidden supply of the most desired brands, Prada, Gucci, Hermes, Chanel and Dior.

"These bags not kept here anymore, madam. Show me what you want, I bring for you …"

After choosing, the next task was haggling over price, the bit Daniella found the hardest. But she'd learnt to play hard to get the best bargain, and so they went back and forth until a price was settled: a hundred dirhams more than she thought they should pay, but a thousand less than the man had initially said, so she was satisfied.

"Four Mulberry bags for less than two hundred quid is a bargain," said Katie as they walked away, attempting to find a restaurant she'd read about along 'curry corridor'. Daniella smiled at her friend. Katie's sun-tanned face was aglow, her cheeks flushed a pretty pink from their shopping trip, eyes shiny and round from the rush of pleasure. Before Daniella could reply, another man appeared from out of the shadows and tried to convince them to get into his car. "Come," he beckoned. "I take you. Best prices."

Daniella grabbed Katie's arm, and they strode on, the plastic bag containing their purchases bumping against her leg.

As Daniella's taxi approached Karama, an image of Katie's excited face swam before her eyes. Her shopaholic friend had told her at breakfast she was going back to Karama. She'd made the announcement as though electricity had just swept through her. Daniella decided not to come. Now she wished more than anything that she had gone. She wasn't convinced that, without her there, Katie would have the good sense to not get into a salesman's car by herself. She was terrified that, in pursuit of the bargains laid out like breadcrumbs, her friend may have been led deeper into Karama and into some kind of serious trouble.

Katie

Katie handed over a hundred-dirham note and stuffed the plastic bag inside a much bigger carrier bag. She hadn't meant to buy sunglasses too, but she loved the tortoiseshell rims, oversize lenses and gold-plated arms on her new Ray-Bans. It was important to take care of your eyes, and Dubai was so sunny, the whole city bathed in a warm, golden glow that reflected off the buildings and cars. She *needed* another pair of sunnies. A spare pair.

Continuing down the street, she totted up everything she'd spent on holiday so far. Her biggest buy, of which she was most pleased, was the Oriental rug in rich reds and blues; it had resembled a flying carpet and she'd known instantly it would look perfect in her living room, once it arrived. If it arrived. The seller had taken her money and address, and arranged shipping.

Then there was the cashmere pashmina from the textile souk, so soft it could have been handspun by angels; the pink teardrop earrings from the Marina Market, which she'd worn to bed without turning her ears green (should have bought the hoops too), and the cushions and Arabic lantern from Global Village.

There was the plush, cuddly camel, but that was a present for her niece so it didn't count. Same went for the chocolate dates; they were a gift for her mother. Okay, so she'd had to buy them twice as she'd eaten the first box late one night. She glanced down at her feet, slapping against the pavement, and remembered that she'd also acquired her sparkly flip flips in Dubai … Maybe she had spent quite a lot.

She blamed it on not being familiar with the money. It was like monopoly money – too easy to hand over, and her conversions into pounds deliberately on the low side. *I should call it a day, go back to Daniella's. Have a swim on her rooftop and a lounge around before cocktails and dinner.*

Turning her mind to what to wear that evening, she decided to have a quick drink before getting a taxi. She was parched from walking around in the heat. She hadn't noticed how thirsty she was while shopping, but now that the exhilaration was over it was as though a hangover was creeping in. Ducking into a restaurant, she put her bags down carefully on a chair and ordered a diet Pepsi. By the time it came, she felt a little restored just from sitting in the air-conditioning. Ice cubes clinked against the glass as she took a long, satisfying sip. She finished her drink quickly and looked up, straight into the face of a fair-haired man standing by her table. He raised a hand in greeting and smiled.

"Sorry to interrupt," he said. "I think we're staying in the same building … Tecom Two Towers?"

"Yes, that's right," said Katie pleasantly enough, although she was a little surprised he'd approached her so directly. She didn't recognise him at all. He had tanned, chiseled features, dominated by piercing ice-blue eyes that either looked cold, wanting or a little too intense.

"You on holiday here?" he asked, smiling easily at her again, not seeming to notice her reservation.

"I am … I come every year, to see my best friend." She stirred the melting ice cubes in the bottom of her glass with the straw.

"So you've done all the tourist hot spots, then?"

She nodded then after a pause asked if he was also on vacation. He shook his head, his gaze boring into her. "No, business. I'm just killing time between meetings. Thought I'd get myself a new watch. I heard there were some great bargains to be had in Karama."

"Find anything?" she asked, perking up.

"Still looking. How about you? Anything good?" He eyed her bags and then said, "Looks like you've been successful."

"Yes," she replied happily, warming to him. If he was trying to chat her up, he was doing a jolly good job by showing an interest in her shopping spree. She gave a brief rundown of where she'd been, the watches he should look at, and when he didn't change the subject she told him all about the best place she'd visited; an upstairs office where a filing cabinet was pushed aside to give access to a larger area of knock-off merchandise. "But good stuff. You know – real fakes," she joked, mimicking the salesman.

A cold feeling suddenly crept over her. This man was too good to be true. Men were never this interested in shopping. *He must be an undercover cop.* Why hadn't she realised sooner?

"Mind if I join you for a drink? I'm Nick, by the way."

She flinched. She was convinced now she was about to get arrested. But he couldn't be. The hair colour was all wrong. He sounded Australian, his accent clipped, his vowels turned on their head. He looked nothing like the police officers she'd seen patrolling Jumeriah Beach Road in a green-and-white Lamborghini Aventador. Maybe he was from Interpol?

"I'm sorry," said Nick after an awkward silence. He took a small step backwards. "I didn't mean to put you in an awkward spot. I thought … Look, I'll just go."

"No," Katie heard herself saying. "I thought you were a policeman."

He threw his head back and laughed.

Two coffees later, they paid the bill and walked out into the bright sunshine. Katie was intending to take Nick to a store where she'd seen a wide selection of watches, but quickly became disorientated. The low-rent suburb of Karama was one of the least exclusive shopping destinations in Dubai, with ugly, inner-city, 1970s low-rise apartment blocks and ethnic eateries lining the dusty streets. She was sure they were in the right area, but something wasn't right.

"Can you remember the name?" asked Nick.

Katie shook her head regretfully. "We could go to the Gold Souk. There's plenty of watches there," she said, feeling in her pocket for a card given to her by a taxi driver the day before. She fished it out. "Have you got time?"

He checked his watch. "Sure."

"It'll be quicker in a taxi – this guy was slightly odd but said he'd be available today to run me anywhere I wanted to go … anytime. I'll call him. Then he can take me back to Tecom." She let out a suppressed giggle. "Or Barsha Heights, as it's now called, isn't it?"

Daniella

"Mrs Todd, hello," said the police officer. He raised the crime scene tape for her to pass under. Daniella's heart was beating in her stomach, and she thought she might vomit.

"No, no, it's not what you think," said the policeman, his forehead reddening. "We raided this place earlier this week, he explained, proudly pointing out the damage where they'd had to prise open a sealed shop front. "Come, there's someone upstairs who might be able to help."

Daniella ducked under the cordon and stared up at a nondescript address in the middle of an old Karama cluster. The building staring back at her was particularly unkempt, a pile of bricks outside begging to be cleared; its dark, rectangular windows quite unlike the arched cut-outs of the neighbouring structures.

She followed the police officer inside and up a staircase that climbed away into a dismal gloom. Her companion flicked a torch on, and in the pool of light she counted five flats, their doors all shut, plus a meter room, which was open. A bicycle was chained to the rails on the first floor.

At the top of the building, a yellowish light shone from a bare bulb, illuminating a door in need of a new coat of paint. Daniella jumped at the sound of the policeman knocking loudly. Raising his voice, he said something in Arabic through the keyhole.

A dog barked inside.

No-one answered, and he knocked again, harder this time.

A woman, holding a big, black Pit Bull Terrier by its collar, finally opened the door. She eyed the pair suspiciously and blinked rapidly, as if startled. "Not again," she said, and gave a raspy sigh. She had a missing front tooth and grey, wire-wool hair that was bunched in tight curls around an elfin face covered in deep age lines.

"We're looking for someone," said the policeman. "This lady's friend," he said, gesturing to Daniella beside him.

Daniella forced a smile and showed the woman a photo of Katie stored on her phone. A holiday snap, taken at a gastropub where they'd enjoyed free fizz on Ladies Night.

Ar rooff. Straining to leap forward, the dog's fur bristled. Ordinarily she would have petted its head, but it was baring its teeth and she didn't dare.

The woman grabbed for the phone and peered at the screen, then shook her head. She pushed the dog back inside and closed the door with a bang; the noise hit Daniella's ears like a slap in the face, and all that was left was the unmistakable smell of incense.

The policeman shrugged and turned to go back down the stairs. "Let's have a walk around," he suggested.

They rejoined the sprinkling of tourists on Karama's dusty streets, stopping every now and then to show residents Katie's picture. No-one recognised her. Every person they asked gave them a blank look. A firm, resounding head shake. The presence of a uniformed officer sent several shady-looking characters scurrying inside like spiders into a crevice. Not one tout approached them, and Daniella wondered if she'd have better luck without the policeman. *Someone must have seen Katie.* She was so pretty, striking even. Tall and slim. She had the sort of looks that people noticed.

After half an hour of fruitless searching, the tight feeling in Daniella's chest turned into sparks of pain. Fragments of music and conversation littered the streets, and wafts of heavily spiced Indian food blended with the fear rising like bile up her throat. All thoughts led back to something bad, something horrible, happening to her friend.

She recalled the taxi ride they'd taken home the day before, and wondered if she should tell the police officer about the driver. He'd been friendly. Too friendly. He immediately started talking about the awful traffic and how annoying other drivers could be. Tongues had loosened and it seemed no topic was taboo. Before long he started discussing religion, then he moved onto relationships and out came the words they always found difficult to answer: "Are you married?"

Daniella disliked being asked this because people could give such a look of disbelief, concern, sympathy and confusion when she said no.

"Nope, both single," said Katie.

"Are all the men in the UK gay then?" he replied.

Katie laughed and thanked him for the compliment.

Despite his humour, they could see he was struggling to understand why two 36-year-old women would be single and weren't surprised when he asked if they'd split up from their partners.

"Broke up with my other half six months go, and on the look out for someone new," said Katie cheerfully.

"Good," he said, "because too long without sex isn't good for anyone."

Daniella had nearly choked on her own tongue. He went on to tell them that people call it love juice but he called it poison and thought you should expel it from your body regularly through good sex. He laughed at his words and they did too, agreeing whole heartedly that sex was healthy and given a choice they would like to find someone to help cleanse their body from the poison within. But, despite the banter, Daniella had climbed out the car feeling uncomfortable.

She was still considering whether to tell the policeman about the taxi driver when a waiter they'd approached told them he was sure he'd served Katie that day.

Daniella's heart leapt into her throat. "Really?"

He nodded. "About four o clock. Told me she was from England, big shopping bags." He spread his arms wide to indicate their size and grinned. "She was with someone, a man."

"A man?" Daniella echoed. Katie hadn't said she was meeting anyone. *She would have told me.*

"Blonde hair," said the waiter. "About my height. I don't remember much else, I'm afraid. They had coffees and left together."

At least someone had seen her. But where she'd gone after that, the waiter had no idea.

Katie

Katie juggled her shopping bags as she rummaged around for her phone. "Where the hell has it got to? Ah, here it is." She frowned, trying to remember what code to use for Dubai and wondering if she'd get through to the taxi driver.

"Let me hold your bags," said Nick.

She'd already resisted his protestations that he could carry something for her ("Looks heavy!" he'd said) and wasn't about to hand over her shopping now. "It's fine, honestly."

Katie had just begun tapping the number in when they were approached by a tout. Persuasive and full of promises, he convinced them to come to his shop rather than go to the Gold Souk.

In a buoyant mood – she was on holiday *and* shopping with a man she'd decided was actually really good-looking – Katie felt like she was bouncing along with a new lightness and revived sense of fun. Even if she never saw Nick again, what did it matter? What harm could visiting one more store with him do? She felt perfectly safe in Karama. This was just turning into her best day on holiday so far.

The salesman helpfully stopped the traffic as he guided them across the road towards a passageway. They turned left at the end, went through a door, and up some stairs to the first floor. Behind another locked door was an enormous Aladdin's cave of goods. Designer bags with gold buckles, zips, silver chain straps, trendy magnetic clasps; sunglasses; belts; shoes – Katie had never seen such a huge collection of counterfeit items.

He quickly produced a tray of watches that weren't on display and invited them to sit down. Nick took far longer bartering than choosing the actual watch, then they were left to their own devices to wander around. Katie suspected their salesman would have followed them up and down the aisles if he hadn't been distracted by the arrival of a German couple, chaperoned by a younger man who rapidly retreated.

"Why is everything in here?" Katie heard a voice ask.

"Because it's illegal," replied the vendor, matter-of-factly. She listened as he told the newcomers the bags were genuine. "Genuine leather," he said, when pressed.

"Ooh, I love this one," said Katie, pointing at a colourful, purple Givenchy leather shoulder bag, her raised arm halting Nick like a stop barrier coming down as she reached for the bag. She drew it to her chest and and felt the soft material between the pads of her fingers. Not wanting to bore her unlikely companion silly, she shoved it back on the shelf and was surprised when she saw Nick standing with his hands against the wall, leaning forwards slightly. What on earth was he doing? He gave her a sidelong glance, a curious look in a face that suddenly appeared sly. He didn't know this place, did he? He'd been doing a jolly good impression of being a first-time visitor.

Before her very eyes, the wall started giving way. Nick placed his hand on a ledge and pushed; a section of wall – with shelves attached – swung backwards easily, opening to reveal an L-shaped room. "Want to see where they keep all the really expensive bags?" he said, turning to face her. "Look inside."

Katie gasped, realising he'd opened a secret door. She stepped in, Nick right behind her, his breath hot on her neck, and felt her eyes widen as she gazed round in awe. This. This was fantastic. Lines of shelves stretched the length of the wall, the off-white wood linear and solid, the handbags piled up in a higgledy-piggledy, careless fashion as though they'd fallen straight off the back of the truck into the room.

They didn't talk – somehow it seemed wrong to break the silence of the inner handbag sanctuary, and anyhow, it all felt terribly naughty. They weren't meant to be here. In this illegal place. Katie browsed, her concentration fully focused on the merchandise, until a loud, clicking noise nearly made her jump out of her skin in fright.

Daniella

Daniella spent a fraught hour in the police station filling in paperwork, then went home around midnight and collapsed onto the sofa, hugging a cushion to her chest. Tears stung her eyes. They were no closer to finding Katie, and she was beside herself with worry. Fear squeezed her lungs and tightened her throat. She looked at her phone on the coffee table like it was a time bomb about to go off. *C'mon Katie. Ring. Please ring.*

The silence was unbearable. It stretched and filled the room, broken only by the sound of her cat meowing for food. Katie's map of Dubai lay on the table, exactly where she'd left it, and Daniella was sure she could smell her floaty perfume, lingering on long after she'd left the apartment on a wave of pre-shopping excitement.

Unable to sit still, Daniella got up and splashed wine into a glass. She took a huge gulp, then set it down on the kitchen counter and wrung her hands. She knew she had to call Katie's mother in the UK.

***

Daniella awoke early in a knot of bed sheets after just a few fitful hours of sleep. Following the initial half-second of memory loss gifted to the newly traumatised, she checked her phone, leapt out of bed and ran to the spare room. She was convinced Katie would be there. She'd better have a jolly good excuse for turning up in the middle of the night, without getting in contact. Daniella wanted to kill her … except she wasn't there. The bed was unslept in, the sheets still crisp, the pillow untouched. A flush raced up her neck and anxiety curled in her stomach like spoilt milk.

Remembering with a sharp kick that Katie's mother was on her way from Heathrow, she picked up her phone again to re-read her message: "On first available flight. Arriving 10.45". Telling Janice, neurotic at the best of times, had been terrible. No mother should ever have to be told that her offspring was missing in the Middle East. Katie's mum probably thought her daughter had been sold into slavery.

She called the police station – no news. They'd ring as soon as they had any updates, they told her and abruptly hung up.

Daniella flung clothes on, made coffee, and sat at the table, her head in her hands, wondering what the hell to do next? It wasn't even six in the morning. The first pale fingers of dawn were creeping through the windows, rendering the light in the room grey and grainy. The day stretched out ahead of her like a tightrope over a gaping canyon. *Think! Think! What to do?*

She couldn't stand the waiting. Grabbing her iPad, she pulled up Facebook, on the remote chance that Katie had posted something. The latest photo hadn't changed – Katie's smiling face beamed at her from the picture, taken on Kite Beach on a glorious day.

The minutes crawled by like hours, the hours like days. She rang a friend in desperation and drank too much coffee, eventually leaning her forehead against the hard table. She closed her eyes, wishing she could turn back time and accompany Katie to Karama.

Her phone rang at about quarter to eight.

It was Katie.

By now she'd drunk so much coffee that her pulse was flying. She answered the call with trembly fingers, nearly dropping the phone as adrenaline surged through her body.

"Shit, Katie, thank God. Are you okay? Where the fuck are you?"

"Yes, I'm fine."

Relief washed over her like floodwater. "Jesus Christ. WHAT THE HELL HAPPENED?"

"I'm so sorry, I can explain everything. You won't believe it actually. I'm still in Karama."

The line crackled and Daniella heard her talking to a taxi driver. "Tecom Towers ... yes that's right." She thought she heard another man's voice, an Australian accent.

"Who's that Katie? Who are you with?"

"That's Nick. I'll explain ... I'll see you in twenty."

The line went dead and Daniella didn't know whether to be ecstatically happy or white hot with anger.

Katie arrived just as Daniella got off the phone with Katie's sister. She was clutching her shopping bags. Heavy-lidded panda eyes suggested she hadn't slept much. But she looked okay. More than okay actually. She looked like the cat that had got the cream, not the thin, skinny version but the delicious, full-fat, mouth-watering froth. Daniella rushed over and hugged her. A blonde, slightly disheveled man stood in the doorway.

"This is Nick – he's staying two floors up," said Katie, sheepishly. "I said we'd make him some breakfast. It's the least I can do." She chuckled. They gave each other a smile that seemed far too intimate for two people who yesterday were strangers.

"We got locked in a secret handbag room," explained Katie. "God knows where – we'd probably never be able to find the place again. We sort of stumbled in, literally. Had to spend the night there as the staff went home. They only discovered us this morning."

Nick shrugged and twisted his mouth into a grimace. "Yep – all night. In a room full of handbags."

"Come in," Daniella said to Nick. She turned back to Katie. "Are you serious? I thought you'd been murdered. I honestly thought you were dead." She groaned and exhaled through her nose. "I got the police involved ... Your mother's coming."

Katie's eyes widened. "Oh God."

"Why didn't you call?"

"No signal."

"I've been so worried about you. I've barely slept."

"I'm so, so sorry." Katie had visibly paled. "Is she on a plane?"

"Yes … Your sister has sent her a text but she won't get it until she lands. We're trying to get a message to her via the airline."

"Oh God," said Katie again. "What a terrible mess. Mum must have been–"

"Distraught. Yes," said Daniella, nodding solemnly. "So was I."

Katie lowered her eyes, silenced for once, the smile wiped off her face and replaced with a stricken look. She was close to tears now.

"It was my fault," said Nick, clearing his throat so his voice didn't sound quite so husky and low. "I noticed a secret door and pushed it open. The room was crammed full, stacked to the rafters with stock." He glanced at Katie, worry stamped all over his face, then raised an eyebrow. "As you can imagine, Kate was–"

"In her element," Daniella finished for him. She could just imagine her best friend exploring the inner handbag sanctuary, abuzz with adrenaline, poring over the bags like a tanned daddy-long-legs. Shopping had always been her favourite drug.

"The handbags were piled up so high," said Katie, rallying. "The stock needed a good sort out." Her mouth twitched upwards. "Honestly, it was more fun than Ladies Night. You should have been there … "

Daniella glared at her friend, incredulous.

Katie swallowed and rearranged her face into a serious expression. "When we went back to the door, we couldn't open it from the inside. Broke my fingernails trying to prise it open," she said, holding her hands up, as if trying to prove how hard they'd tried. She dropped her arms back to her side. "We knocked and yelled for help, but no one came. We had no choice but to spend the night … "

Nick and Katie exchanged a stolen, lingering glance.

"So sorry Dani."

"Really am sorry," said Nick, red in the face, "to have caused such distress."

The pair spoke at once.

Please, thought, Daniella, spare me the details.

"I'll make it up to you all, I promise," said Katie. "And mum, when she arrives. Here … have this," she said, reaching into one of her carrier bags and pulling out a cerise pink handbag with gold stitching. "I used it as a pillow, and they let me have it to say sorry. I know it doesn't let me off the hook for what I've just put you through … but it is …" She squeezed the handbag one last time and then offered it to Daniella as though it were an olive branch. "… Michael Kors."

The Big-Ticket Present

There were only a few vehicles in the staff car park when Hilary pulled up in her battered Peugeot. The headmistress wanted to see her before the start of the teaching day, and so Hilary had set her alarm for five thirty.

    Yawning, she pulled her metallic silver sunshade out of its pouch and attached it to the windshield, as though she was blindfolding the glass. Then she stepped out into the heat of the morning, locking her car with a click.

    The air was already heavy, thick with a cloying humidity that would turn her vehicle into an oven by the time she returned to it. This happened every day during the last month of term, even with the deflective sunshade. For some reason, June's steep rise in temperature surprised her every year – probably because the climate was so different from the fresh, pure air of the Welsh highlands, where they still owned a cottage. Summer in the desert had a tendency to leave Hilary feeling as though she was breathing through hot, sticky treacle.

Beads of perspiration formed in the fine lines on her forehead and between her shoulder blades as she walked to the main building's wide, glass doors. The lobby, in contrast, was blissfully cool and she took a moment to enjoy the feel of the air-conditioning hitting her skin. She wiped the back of her hand across her forehead, checked the time, and strode to the headmistress's office.

Hilary had no idea what she'd been summoned for. She imagined it might be about Sami, her most challenging pupil, who she'd recommended should repeat the year despite her best efforts to bring him up to speed with the rest of Y2 Yellow.

She knocked on the head's door and from within heard a terse "come in". Had she got the day wrong? No, she'd definitely said Tuesday. Hilary pushed the door open.

It was a room she'd sat in many times before during her ten years at the school, a room certain students only knew with fear and respect. Mrs Claute was formidable. She didn't tolerate rule-breakers. Each time Hilary attended meetings in this office, she couldn't help noticing that the books and spiky plants pushed against the window looked as though they were seeking an escape from the narrow ledge.

Mrs Claute didn't look up immediately, and when she did it was with a tight smile. "Ah yes," she said, setting the manila folder she'd been reading from down. She was sitting on a high-backed chair behind a huge, solid mahogany desk with a computer on one side. "Take a seat," she said, gesturing to a swivel armchair. Mrs Claute closed the folder and pushed her glasses back up the bridge of her nose. "I'm just going through the paperwork from our inspection."

Hilary gave her a half smile and inwardly grimaced, remembering the effort it had taken to maintain the school's outstanding rating. She'd stayed up late tweaking lesson plans and making teaching aids, then came in early to find a team of men painting outside her classroom. She'd been a ball of stress that week, the profit-making school turned into a set to impress the inspectors and the teachers the theatre artists.

"I can imagine it's scintillating reading," Hilary said, and immediately regretted it when Mrs Claute didn't respond.

They'd even had props (new sports equipment that promptly disappeared afterwards) and laid on extra Arabic classes to impress the authorities. She'd gritted her teeth and gone along with it, as she did every year, knowing it could be worse: at their sister school, they'd devised a scheme to give the teacher a cue in the presence of the inspectors. Students who knew the answer raised their right hand, while those who didn't put up their left hand.

"Next year …" said Mrs Claute, breaking the awkward silence, "… we'll get the parents more involved." She peered through her glasses. Hilary watched her boss's eyebrows move up and down as she talked about planting mums under palm trees outside to read to the kids; dads doing power-point presentations on leadership.

It hadn't been like this when Hilary had been at the coalface of parenting primary school children almost 20 years ago. School mums took their involvement so seriously now. With their bunched up shoulders. Their class WhatsApp groups. Trotting into school in their gym wear, honeyed highlights glinting in the sun, their smartphones at the ready like lifelines. Always busy, always rushing. Hilary was glad though. It made her job much easier.

"Ready for the holiday?" asked Mrs Claute, briskly changing the subject.

"Definitely. I think everyone is. The children are tired – the heat's getting to everyone."

Mrs Claute picked up a pen. "Are you heading off somewhere nice?"

"I am, yes. My daughter and her new baby are joining us at our home in Wales."

"How lovely. I didn't know you'd become a grandmother."

Hilary felt a surge of pride well up inside her. "Yes, two weeks ago," she said proudly. Not that she'd actually met her granddaughter yet. Skype was a poor substitute for skin-to-skin contact with the cutest grandbaby she'd ever laid eyes on. But Y2 Yellow needed her too, and it had all happened so close to the end of term. She'd meet her in six days' time and could barely contain her excitement.

Mrs Claute clicked the lid shut on her silver fountain pen and set it down. She glanced at the clock. "I don't want to keep you too long Hilary … but we've been contacted by one of the dads in your class." She hesitated. "Malik's dad."

Hilary hid a jolt of surprise. "Oh," she said. She'd always had a lot more to do with his wife – his wife number three to be exact – than the father, who was an important member of Dubai's ruling family and had only been seen in the school once. He was a trim man, in a white kandora, spotlessly laundered and smooth amid the ink-stained school uniforms. They'd had a brief, polite conversation, watched over by a bodyguard, before he'd left with his son.

Malik's mother, on the other hand, was a regular in the classroom. She'd drift in on a gust of perfumed opulence, Kohl-eyed and graceful, the train of her black abaya trailing over the playground. They'd struck up something of a professional friendship during their sessions discussing her son's progress.

"How is Malik getting on?" asked Mrs Claute.

"Very well now. He's come on tremendously."

Mrs Claute nodded. On her face was a stern, flinty expression that recalled her long career as a headmistress. "Yes, I know you've been tutoring him out of hours."

Hilary pictured Malik, the curve of his olive cheeks; those rosebud lips, his uncomplicated eyes – deep pools of melted brown chocolate that followed her around the classroom. She was fond of him. He'd needed a lot of help with English, and basic numeracy, but had blossomed under her tutelage.

His mother, from Jordan, was beautiful and devoted to her only child. Her face had lit up when she'd told her Malik was now right where he should be academically. She'd clapped her jewelled fingers together in delight and tapped her toes – which Hilary noticed were encased in shiny baby-pink Manolo Blahnik heels, peeking out from underneath sequined black folds of cloth.

"I'm glad to hear it," Mrs Claute continued. Her tone had become even more businesslike. "The reason I wanted to meet with you this morning is that his father wants to give you a present – for your efforts." She emphasised the word 'present' with a raise of the eyebrows, but it was as though she was speaking through clenched teeth.

Mrs Claute cleared her throat. "The gift is a Range Rover."

Hilary's heart gave a single big thump. A Range Rover? *Did she hear that right?* For a moment, she was speechless, and then sensed an acrimonious feeling rushing in around them, filling the room with its uneasiness. "Goodness," she blurted out. "That's terribly generous … I don't quite know what to say." Her hand flew to her mouth.

She'd never won anything big in her life, and imagined that this must be what it would be like to match up the winning numbers with a lottery ticket, or snag a big-ticket item at a raffle. The bare skin on her arms prickled against the chilled air, a tingly feeling heightened by a surge of adrenalin. Her heart clattered in her chest and her lungs felt like they'd been filled to capacity.

"There's a problem though," Mrs Claute said, lowering her eyes. When she looked up, she clasped her hands together and laid them on the desk in front of her. She looked like she was about to break bad news. Hilary was sure she saw a flicker of – what was it? – barely concealed jealousy pass over the headmistress's mask-tight features.

She felt her own face quickly run through a series of emotions, the initial surprise giving way first to wariness, and then to the kind of disappointment a lottery winner might feel on not being able to find the ticket. She realised she was holding her breath.

"I'm afraid …" said Mrs Claute, "… due to school policy on gifts of excessive monetary value, we can't allow you to accept the car."

"Oh," said Hilary, expelling the air from her lungs and feeling as deflated as a balloon that had popped and was fizzling back to earth.

"I'm sure you'll understand. I can't allow anything that would jeopardise our next inspection … So I'll need you to very politely decline their gesture, without causing offence, of course," said Mrs Claute with a benign smile.

***

"Seriously?" gasped Blanche, her eyes widening. "A Range Rover?" They were alone in the staffroom, and Hilary had decided to confide in her friend, a year five teacher. She hadn't told anyone yet – she was trying to pretend she didn't mind, when really the headmistress's curt words were ringing in her ears like tinnitus.

The room was filled with the yellow sunlight of a blazing-hot morning. On a side counter there was a kettle next to a collection of bright ceramic mugs and a plate of Rich Tea biscuits. As she told Blanche not to get too excited – she wouldn't actually *get* the car – her friend's eyes clouded over.

Blanche turned the tap on hard to wash a mug, the water blasting noisily into the sink. She shook her head slowly. "Silly woman, that Mrs Claute," she said a little too loudly. Hilary's gaze shot to the door, as though the head might walk in any minute. "I bet she's green with envy," Blanche continued. "She still hasn't forgiven you for showing her up in that meeting with Sami's parents. You've done so much for Malik – and anyway, it's not like his dad can't afford it."

"True," said Hilary, thinking about the royal family's fleet of super cars; their enormous royal yacht, as big as a block of flats; their private jets. They could easily afford it. She flicked the kettle on, and peered into her cup at the teabag's papery, perforated skin.

"Anyway …" she sighed "… teachers' gifts are getting out of hand. All these expensive spa vouchers, Swarovski jewellery. Parents these days are just trying to outdo each other. I've been saying that for the past few years, so it would be hypocritical to accept the car, even if I was allowed to."

She cast her mind back to when she began teaching thirty years ago. "I remember a time when children used to just make something, or pick flowers on the way to school."

Blanche shrugged. "How many kids actually walk to school here? Very few," she said, getting the milk out of the fridge. She pushed the refrigerator door shut firmly. "They're driven – in big cars! Did you hear that Carol, in year six, got asked by the mums if she wanted to pick out some furniture?"

Hilary shook her head lamely, wondering if that was allowed.

"Besides, we do far more than just teach these days. Admin work, after-school activities, weekend workshops – we're expected to do it all," Blanche grumbled. "You wouldn't catch me turning down a Tiffany bracelet or Mulberry handbag." She jutted her chin in defiance. "Tell me … why is it okay for a business man to treat potential clients to fancy dinners and presents, but not okay for parents to give nice gifts to teachers?"

Hilary poked her friend gently in the ribs. "Well you're in the right city for over-the-top gestures," she said, smiling at the twinkle in her friend's eye. Blanche always made her chuckle, even if she could be quite outrageous at times.

"Let's see what a business client thinks of a handmade card!" said Blanche with a snort.

They poured the tea, and sat down on the comfy sofa, sinking in to its soft cushions. Hilary nibbled a biscuit, a crumb falling from the corner of her mouth, while Blanche leafed through a tatty copy of *Grazia*. A Range Rover. Top-of-the-line. Leather seats, LCD screens, and that new-car smell. Would have been nice, she mused. *Oh well.* Another thought struck her as the disappointment began to pinch like a stitch in her side: *What on earth will I tell John tonight?* Her husband had been talking about buying a new car for months.

***

"What do you mean you're not allowed to keep it?" exclaimed John that evening, after getting in late, tired and hot from work. He loosened his tie and unbuttoned his collar, visibly cooling after an uncomfortable walk from the Metro. His jacket was slung over his arm, revealing sweat circles under his armpits.

"After all the extra hours you've put in. Evenings. Weekends. That bloody woman's got a lot to answer for. What's it got to do with *her*, anyway?"

"She said the only way I could keep the car was if I resigned," Hilary replied. She continued stacking the dishwater with gusto, plates clanking as she moved dishes and bowls around inside to make room.

"Well–"

"I can't John, you know that. I love my job, I'm not ready to give it up yet."

"You could get a job at another school. Or retire? Isn't it time to stop working so hard? C'mon love, give it some thought. You deserve to enjoy yourself more, rather than working your socks off." He said it gently, but it wasn't what she wanted to hear.

Hilary straightened up to cast him a look, staring hard at his chest as she struggled with her annoyance. At 53, she wasn't ready to retire, and starting somewhere new was the last thing she wanted to do. Anyway, if she did change jobs, she'd been beginning to think she might like to do something to help less privileged children. Give something back. She'd been so blessed with two beautiful daughters, and now a healthy granddaughter too. She shouldn't have told John about the car.

"That old Peugeot of yours isn't going to last much longer, you know," he said, a ruddy colour flaring in his cheeks, "and the garage called today to say my Explorer needs four new tyres."

Hilary looked away, and rinsed a dirty pan under the cold tap's sun-warmed water, while John left the kitchen to shower.

Lost in her thoughts, the doorbell startled her. Hilary's slippers slapped against the marble floor as she padded over to the door. It seemed a little late for visitors. It was gone nine pm, and she was already thinking about bed. Holding the brass handle, she pulled the door open and breathed in the still-stifling heat.

Malik's mother stood in the porch, silhouetted by the street lamp, her abaya as black as the night. Beyond the iron railings of their gate, Hilary could see a Lexus with dark, tinted windows, a driver inside. The statuesque woman smiled serenely, her beauty as lovely as the pale half-crescent moon and the scent of next-door's frangipani in the soupy, evening air.

"Aliyah, hi," said Hilary, taken aback.

"Pleez, forgive me," said the woman, "for disturbing you so late."

"Come in," said Hilary, stricken with self-consciousness about the untidy state of their villa, and realising, with dismay, that she had no way of letting John know they had a royal visitor. There was a strong chance he would appear semi naked, in his silk-striped dressing gown, hair dripping wet, asking where the hell his clean boxer shorts were.

Aliyah ghosted in behind her, through the hallway and into the lounge, where Hilary motioned to her to take a seat. "Would you like some coffee?" she asked politely.

"Please," said Aliyah, nodding. She rearranged the long, flowing cloth of her garment as she sat, and laid her soft leather handbag down beside her. She wore a black hijab, decorated on one side with a crystal brooch shaped as a bow, the shiny silver bringing out the glitter in the clear stones.

Safely in the kitchen, Hilary fired off a warning text to her husband upstairs, hoping he'd see it, and prepared a tray of coffee and sweet baklavas. She carried it into the lounge and enquired after Malik.

"He's very well," replied Aliyah, and asked about Hilary's family, following the custom in this part of the world to make mutual enquiries about close relatives before getting down to business. Hilary handed her a coffee and she sipped it regally, like a princess, Cartier bracelets glinting on her slim wrist. The flash of bare flesh was the only skin visible other than her immaculate face and hands.

"Mrs Claute tells me," Aliyah said finally, making the head's name sound exotic, "that you're unable to accept our gift to you … it's a great shame. We really wanted to bestow this gift on you for all your hard work with our son. We're so grateful," she said with a smile that stretched to her huge, heavily made-up eyes.

Her long, ebony eyelashes – curled up like waves above cocoa-brown irises – were surely false.

"Thank you," said Hilary, and launched into a poorly rehearsed speech expressing her gratitude for their kindness. "Yes, unfortunately–" She stopped. The sparkle on Aliyah's hijab caught the light as her head turned.

John stood in the doorway, wearing, to Hilary's relief, beige slacks and a crisp, blue shirt. "*Salam alaykum,*" he said, walking in, his arms held at slightly awkward angles, not in a shaking-hands posture but not relaxed either. He sat down opposite their guest and seemed a little unsure where to hold his gaze.

Aliyah greeted him and carried on talking. She had a classy – almost evocative – perfume on, which clouded up around her on each movement. The effect was mesmerising. Hilary, unused to seeing Malik's mother outside the classroom, listened intently, while John was agog.

"So what I propose is this," she finished, raising a manicured hand to touch the pearl gleaming on her ear like a dewdrop on a desert rose. "Come to work for my family, as a private tutor, and then …" She paused. "You may keep the car."

She uncrossed her legs and Hilary caught a glimpse of dark navy skinny jeans ending in silver heels. Fumbling in her bag, Aliyah pulled out a business card and handed it over. "Have a think," she said, "and call this number, my direct line."

Aliyah rose to leave, and Hilary and John jumped up. On her way out, her robe swished over the hard floor, creating a breeze as she wafted out; her fragrance hung in the air, filling the house with its power long after she'd left. She turned to wave as she climbed into the Lexus, smiling broadly. "Thank you again," she called, and Hilary knew her mind was made up.

***

Under a pale blue sky, builders painted the last remaining wall of the new classrooms at Nchumba Primary School, ready for the hundreds of children who would fill the buildings with chatter and giggles the next day.

All around, it looked like the vegetation had exploded with growth. Hilary stood in the shade, an umbrella of green leaves rustling above her head. Giant baobab trees dotted the landscape and the horizon was a series of purply-green peaks that blended into wispy clouds. In the distance, she could also see stretches of open savanna where the forest thinned to nothing.

The school had been built for just 25 students seven years ago; by 2016 it had 350 pupils, crammed into five classrooms. Three were constructed from planks and had gaping holes in their structure, through which rain trickled in. Some of the surplus children had been studying in huts made from sticks and mud, which could now be torn down.

Hilary stood still admiring the project she'd funded by selling the Range Rover and buying a much cheaper, second-hand model. She only had a week's leave in Kenya, while Malik and his mother travelled to London. But it was enough time to oversee the arrival of new books and equipment, as well as the unveiling of three additional latrines. The smell of new paint filled her lungs, and she pinched the soft inner flesh of her arm, unable to believe it had all come together so well. She was pretty sure that when Aliyah got back from their shopping trip, she'd agree to arrange some on-going funding for the school's future expansion.

Pulling out her iPhone, she snapped some more photos to send to Blanche whenever she next came across internet access. She smiled to herself as she noticed the last picture Blanche had sent her – a gold Tiffany bracelet, still in its box. Her friend had finally been gifted an expensive piece of jewellery, but she wasn't going to keep it. *I've tried it on and it's gorgeous,* Blanche texted, *but I want you to give it to Nchumba Primary's headmistress next time you're in Kenya. Miss you at school. Good luck for the opening x.*

To Slide or Not to Slide?

By Inessa Jackson and Marianne Makdisi

The deck swayed under her as Eugene flopped back into a pool lounger. The sunscreen she'd applied before leaving the cabin had smudged her sunglasses and when she sipped her Tutti Frutti, the tiny pink umbrella wedged itself up her nose.

Sun bit into her leathery arms as her eyes travelled up the colourful tube winding in circles above the pool. The water looks so nice and cool, she thought. And that waterslide would be fun. *I wonder what Richard would think…?* Her husband's smiling face flashed into her mind, but was shoved aside by the vision of ringleader Rosemary's scowling eyebrows.

I'd love to try it, but the ladies would never approve. They'd tut-tut me and what if I had to spend this cruise all alone? She couldn't risk being shunned from her group. Having spent most of her adult life working as a clerk at the Family Court of Australia and then moving across the country to a town where Richard had always wanted to spend his retirement, she'd arrived in her seventies without many close friends. Her daughter – who'd relocated to the UAE six years ago – finally bullied her into a cruise around the Gulf with her local Rotary club a year after Richard passed away.

Fiddling with the collar of her pink moomoo, she absorbed the kids' joyful faces as they popped out the bottom of the waterslide. Eyes wide with glee, mouths open in laughter, they splashed into the pool with delighted squeals. Eugene sat transfixed, listening to the muffled screams inside the tube. The sound called to her, pulled at her heart … *Just a moment to feel young again.*

***

Eugene looked up from her cards straight into Rosemary's piercing, crystal-blue eyes. She wondered if the ship had been swaying more than usual this morning because one of her penciled-on eyebrows was perched higher than the other.

Rosemary placed a queen face-up on the table. "So Eugene, will you be joining us at the scrapbooking session after lunch? Keepsakes must be stored properly, you know."

Lorraine and Betty's silver heads nodded in silent agreement.

She glanced out the window at the churning ocean and focused on the lively white caps that topped the surface like frosting. The emerald waters of the Gulf stretched endlessly in all directions. "I'd love to," she said. Picking up a card from the pile, she tried to push the waterslide from her mind. An echo of the children's laughter and shrieks tickled her ears.

"I'd also love to sit by the pool again this afternoon," she blurted. "It's so sunny up there. And…" she swallowed loudly, "that waterslide looks like fun." Silence struck the table. She stole a look up just as Rosemary's misaligned eyebrows snapped together.

Eugene's heart pounded once, twice. Then Rosemary snorted so violently a cocktail napkin fluttered across the table and sent the top card of Eugene's canasta pile spinning. "My dear, you're such a comedian!"

Eugene tried to smile. "Well, I—"

"Please, STOP, you're too much!" Titters from the other ladies confirmed her comedy skills. "But if there's one thing I know, it's that I'd never have booked this cruise if I'd known it would be overrun by those horrible, noisy kids.

Lorraine and Betty nodded their tightly permed curls.

"They should take that nasty waterslide down before it wrecks anyone else's holiday," Rosemary finished.

"Yes, they do make a bit of a racket I suppose," Eugene mumbled.

***

The next day, Eugene boarded the coach with a wiggle of her wonky hip and sat down by the window. Rosemary got on a few seconds later, wearing a straw sun hat, elasticated slacks, socks and sandals. She hovered beside Eugene's row, waiting for her to move her bag, then plonked herself down in the empty seat. Rosemary removed her hat and patted her hair with a sigh. "I suppose we should do this," she grumbled. "I'd honestly rather stay on the boat."

"You would?" said Eugene, surprised. She'd heard Oman, with its mountain ranges and old-world appeal, was one of the best places in the Gulf to experience traditional Arabia, and had no intention of missing their Muscat city tour.

Rosemary nodded. "I did not like *Doo-bye* one bit," she said, mispronouncing it despite spending two full days in the emirate. She shuddered. "Ghastly place. All those flashy buildings. Everything bigger, better, higher. *Pah!*" A tutting noise escaped her mouth. "An environmental disaster with zero culture. I don't know how your daughter can stand to live there."

"Actually she's very happy. The kids especially love it. Anyway, I think you'll find Oman is quite different from the UAE."

But Rosemary wasn't listening. She was trying to get the attention of the tour guide. "What time will we be back on board?" she trilled.

"About six," he replied, flashing a mega-watt smile.

"Jolly good," said Rosemary. "In time for bingo."

As the coach set off, Eugene thought about her daughter and grandkids, and felt a warm glow fill the empty space in her chest as she counted the days until she'd next see them. Just four more days on the cruise, then she was spending a whole week with them in Dubai.

She'd been terribly upset when they'd moved overseas, and spent the first twelve months waiting for them to come back. Her first visit to the Middle East had been overwhelming. Plucked from a comfortable life of sandwiches and soup in front of the TV with Richard, both wearing slippers, and dropped into a non-stop whirl of champagne brunches, five-star beach clubs, school runs on twelve-lane highways and trips to malls bigger than her home town, it was no wonder she'd had culture shock. The jetlag had hit her so bad, she'd been convinced she had flu.

But as time went by, and she became proficient at Facebook and Skype, she grew more and more proud of her daughter for thriving in her new life, and began to look forward to their annual holidays to the UAE. The travel was so much easier when Richard was alive, though. How she wished they'd also visited Oman together when they'd had the chance. *We always thought we'd have more time.*

Driving through the old port of Muttrah, Eugene admired the rows of traditional white homes with their intricately carved balconies, stained glass art and elegant eaves. Topped with minarets, Muttrah stretched along an attractive corniche, enclosed by a serrated crescent of rust-coloured mountains. The view was dramatic. The tour guide pointed out Sultan Qaboos' superyacht, moored in the harbour, and Eugene was amazed to see it was bigger than the new block of apartments at the end of her road. The yacht even contained a concert hall to accommodate a large symphonic orchestra.

"Streuth," said Rosemary. "How very over the top."

They drove on to the Royal Opera House, built from Omani desert-rose stone, then continued to the magnificent, sandstone Sultan Qaboos Grand Mosque. It was famous, their guide told them, for the enormous eight-and-a-half-tonne chandelier hanging inside. They'd been pre-warned about being modestly dressed, and Eugene whipped out her scarf to cover her hair. Rosemary's face dropped on discovering she'd forgotten hers.

"Not a problem," said the guide. "You can hire a scarf over there." He pointed at the gift shop. "They have abayas, too, if you wanted to really look the part."

"Oh I don't think so," Rosemary shot back.

Eugene watched as her friend reluctantly wrapped the folds of black material around her head. Her nose crinkled. "Is it clean?"

The lady helping her either didn't hear, or didn't understand, and Eugene inwardly chuckled, remembering how misinformed Rosemary had been about the Middle East. Rosemary had imagined her daughter must be under all sorts of restrictions in Dubai. *"Does she have to wear a veil?"* she'd enquired, her eyes widening like buttons. *"Can she drive?"* Eugene had half expected her to ask if women had to walk five paces behind their husbands, and risked having their hand chopped off if they got into trouble. *Clueless woman*. She hoped the last person to wear the scarf had lice.

Eugene was right about Oman. The sultanate beat to a leisurely pace; it was spotlessly clean, welcoming and modern, while also being a refreshing reminder of a bygone age. By the time they got back to Muttrah via a wadi lush with trees, grasses and flowering shrubs, she was itching to get off the coach again and explore. She wanted to immerse herself in the corniche on foot, and get away from Rosemary, who'd fallen asleep, her mouth gaping open, letting out gaspy, arrhythmic snores.

They were dropped just outside the ancient Muttrah souk, opposite the harbour. Inside, Eugene gazed at the colourful stalls set up beneath gorgeous Islamic architecture. All around her hawkers touted their wares; sumptuous pashminas, gold jewellery, frankincense, spices and perfumes. Exotic smells drifted over and Eugene soaked up the atmosphere, alert to the calls of the shopkeepers and the fragments of foreign languages spoken by passers-by. Determined to make sense of the maze and escape Rosemary's complaints about her blisters, she ventured away from the touristy main drag into the labyrinth of backstreets, and lost not only her friend, but also all track of time.

Rosemary's eyes shot daggers at her as she climbed the steps into the coach. She was a few minutes late, and they were all waiting for her. Thirty blank faces stared at her as she walked up the aisle, her cheeks aflame from rushing and the embarrassment. Circles of perspiration soaked her blouse.

"What happened to you?" hissed Rosemary. "We all managed to get back here twenty minutes ago."

The air-conditioning pumped out a frigid draught, and Eugene pretended she needed to sit for a minute to cool off before she could talk.

***

At the dinner buffet, Eugene spread butter across her sweetcorn. "Tut tut. Looks like *someone* won't fit into their bathing costume for the rest of their holiday," said Rosemary. She slurped her drink and added, "and no more babbling about that waterslide please."

Eugene swallowed down the lump in her throat. "It's just a bit of fun, isn't it?"

"Fun? The ladies of Bondi Junction Rotary Club will NOT be seen sliding in public! Good grief Mrs Potter, what would people say?" Rosemary scoffed.

Staring at her plate, Eugene said in a soft voice, "I don't really mind what they say."

A slop of liquid escaped Rosemary's cup as she jerked upright in her chair. "Rubbish," she said, her eyes travelling up and down Eugene. "Plus, you'd frighten the children. No one wants to see a seventy-something grandmother bellyflop into the pool."

Eugene sat back and let the sway of the ship calm her thudding pulse. The sweetcorn had turned to cold, wet mush in her mouth. Richard's kind eyes sprang into her mind and she fought to hold back tears. *I miss you, and the fun we had together.* She thought about her daughter's advice to move on, find herself a new life, new people, new adventures. Cherish and live each day. But all she felt was alone.

She looked up to find Rosemary and the ladies standing behind their chairs, glaring down at her. "Well? Eugene? Are you coming? Bingo starts in five minutes, please don't make us late."

***

Eugene arrived on the pool deck the next morning just after sunrise. The first orange-hued rays of sunlight picked out a burnished sheen on the sea, and filled the sky with a pale, pure light. A seagull overhead soared on a thermal. Her hands gripped the salty railing as she looked around for the ladies. Seniors' aqua aerobics had already started. As she dumped her towel on a pool lounger — and kicked off her flip-flops — she caught a glimpse of the waterslide. The line hadn't started yet. All the kids must still be at breakfast.

"COME ON EUGENE! TIME FOR HUFFY PUFFY!" Rosemary screeched from the pool, where lines of over-inflated blow-up dolls bobbed in the swirling water to Whitney Houston.

Eugene filled her lungs with tangy sea air as she approached the side of the pool. "No, thank you Rosemary," she said. "I won't be joining you. There's something else I'd like to do."

"What!? You're not going to exercise? But Eugene, look at yourself!"

Eugene's polite smile slid off her face. "Sorry, Rosemary, look at me how?"

"All that roast you scoffed at the Captain's buffet last night! For mercy's sake, those calories aren't going to burn themselves off."

Eugene glanced down at her leathery bingo wings and wobbly tummy-rolls. Richard had never minded her carrying a bit extra. In fact, he'd liked it. He had often said her soft, round curves were perfect. He'd loved her *just the way she was.*

She stared into Rosemary's crystalline eyes and felt something deep inside her crack. *How dare she?* Drops of water ran down Rosemary's face and off her jawline. Her chin looked like a shovel, and her hair hung in limp strands like a wet mop. *Why am I wasting my time on this woman?*

Backing away from the pool edge, Eugene snapped, "Stop being such a mean old cow. I've been 'round the block too many times to be bullied by someone like you."

Rosemary's face took on the strangled, disbelieving look of a fish gasping for air. Eugene spun on her heels, waddled over to the bright-red slide and locked eyes with the young crew member stationed at the bottom. She raised an eyebrow and with a surprised grin, he gestured with his thumb. "Go on up."

Eugene didn't look back as she climbed the steps.

Standing at the top of the slide, her heart hammering in her ribs, she paused momentarily to take in the view of the ship's upper deck. From up there, the sprinkling of flowery swimming caps below looked like pops of colour on the pool's sparkling surface. The upturned, expectant faces had blurred. She braced herself. Breathing in deeply, she caught a whiff of chlorine.

The only way was down.

Keeping her eyes open, she pushed off and lay flat on her back. Her neck wanted to bob up, but she forced herself to relax as she gathered speed, through watery twists and turns. At some point, her eyes must have closed, and she surrendered to the thrill factor. Her descent was swift and exhilarating. Wildly slippery. Before she knew it, she'd plunged into the pool with a splash that sent water shooting into her sinuses.

She gulped a breath and heard the sound of enthusiastic hand clapping. Blinking hard, she looked around, and, once her vision had cleared, saw that everyone – bar Rosemary – was beaming at her. Lorraine and Betty cheered.

***

Golden sun beat down on Eugene's shoulders as she reclined her pool chair. Warm drips trickled down from her hair, now drying loose around her face. She bunched her moomoo into a pillow and wedged it behind her neck. A smile snuck onto her lips and a wave of something that might be happiness washed over her. She wondered if she might try the slide again the following day, before the pool got busy. How uplifting it had been to feel like a kid again. Even if it had all been over too soon. Heat spread from her stomach down her limbs.

A shadow covered her chest as a man stopped in front of her, blocking the sun. His silhouette reminded her of Paul Newman. Crisp white shirt, silver hair and his eyes wrinkled into mischievous sparkles that complemented his broad smile.

"Yes? Hello," she said, caught off guard by his sudden appearance.

"Pardon for the intrusion. I'm Bryn," he said with another smile. "That looked like fun."

"It was," she nodded, feeling an urge to laugh build inside her. "Eugene." She offered him her hand. Her wet fingers felt wonderfully warm in his palm. "Actually, my friends call me Genie."

"Very nice to meet you Genie … You seem like someone who enjoys adventure."

"Well, I–" She hesitated. "Yes, I do." She'd seen him before. Where was it? The Muttrah Souk, she realised. She'd noticed him buying bright-yellow turmeric at a stall selling fragrant spices.

"In that case," said Bryn, shifting from one foot to the other, "I was wondering if you'd care to join me on deck later for a sunset tango lesson?"

The pent-up chortle escaped her mouth. "I'm sorry," she said quickly. "I didn't mean to laugh. I'm still feeling rather skittish after sliding. That sounds like …" She searched for the right words. "A marvellous idea."

She grinned up at him and, in the corner of her eye, saw Rosemary choking on her mineral water a few chairs away.

The Robot Help

Arabian Ranches, 2020

"Over my dead body," Marcie cried. She fixed her eyes on her husband's face to see if he was serious. Don met her gaze but didn't smile. The crease in his forehead deepened as he took a slurp of tea.

"We've had her for seven years," said Marcie. "We can't just let her go. She's part of our family."

They were standing in the kitchen on a sunny morning. It was vividly bright and the shadows thrown from the palm tree outside cast patterns in the shape of long, spindly fingers on the cream-coloured walls. A stilted silence rushed into the space between them. Don set his mug down on the counter top, a little too sharply, and shrugged.

"Just give it some thought," he appealed. "That's all. It would save us money over the long term."

Marcie heard their housemaid coming through the front door, closing it with a click behind her. "Shh, she's back," she whispered, bringing her index finger to her mouth.

Shopping bags crinkled as Jovilyn carried the groceries into the kitchen and greeted her employers with her usual wide smile. "Hello Sir … Ma'am," she said, nodding. The bags slid from her hands onto the floor, and she began putting everything away as Marcie and Don got ready to head out for work, pretending they hadn't just had a conversation about replacing their housemaid with a robot cleaner.

Of all of Don's hair-brained schemes, this had to be his worst yet, Marcie decided as she drove to her office, still bristling with irritation. It was bad enough every time Jovilyn left for her annual vacation to the Philippines. The first time their live-in helper went on a well-deserved break, Marcie could tell as they said goodbye that she was nervous. She had a long plane journey ahead to Manila, and a ten-hour coach ride to her village. They'd talked about the presents Jovilyn was taking back for her family, then Marcie had realised what she was actually concerned about. Jovilyn had looked at her sagely. "Will you be okay, Ma'am? With the children, by yourself?"

The worry in her eyes was undisguisable. "Of course," Marcie replied, her voice slightly too high. "We'll be absolutely fine. But you will come back, won't you?" she asked with a nervous laugh.

They'd hauled two over-stuffed suitcases outside, then with a swish of her long, black glossy hair, and one last apprehensive glance back, Jovilyn was gone, and Marcie was staring down the barrel of no childcare and a full-time job to hold down for the next month.

Granted the children were growing older and more independent now, but they still needed Jovilyn, still depended on her to make their lives tick over. The robot cleaner they'd seen at the Expo would be a poor substitute for an actual human. What on earth was Don thinking? It was so typical of him. He'd always been obsessed with gadgets. Marcie stared at the flat-screen monitor in the entrance to the parking garage near her office. She pulled onto a pallet platform, got out and locked the car, walking away while motion sensors checked she'd gone and motors began lowering the pallet underground for its ninety-second journey to a parking space.

***

Don had been barely able to contain his excitement at Dubai's much-anticipated 2020 Expo. Technology was his thing, the more futuristic the better, and he'd hardly noticed the crowds that had flocked to the pavilions at the purpose-built site in Jebel Ali. They'd been on their way out, intending to take the new Metro link home, when she'd felt his hand on her arm, steering her towards a zone signposted as an 'Innovation Pod'. Something had caught his eye. "Just quickly," he'd said, sensing she'd had enough of looking at big boys' toys, "then we'll go, I promise."

A throng of people were gathered around a low, flat stage and Marcie had to stand tall just to see, shifting her weight from one foot to the other as heads bobbed in front of her. They were all looking at HouseBOT, a humanoid robot the size of a child of about eight years. Smooth, shiny metal parts slid silently over each other as HouseBOT was put through her paces in a demo that included dusting the wall and carrying a tray of mugs to a table. She completed these tasks with precision, silver and white chrome latched with freely moving connecting rods to lift her arms and legs. The crowd burst into loud, spontaneous applause as HouseBOT lowered her head in an expressionless bow.

Two men wearing headsets moved into the centre of the stage to explain what else the robot could do. Windows, vacuuming, washing-up, sorting laundry – no job was below her; she could even be programmed to garden.

Marcie kept her gaze on HouseBOT, half-expecting her to start turning cartwheels, and noticed a flashing red light behind her lifeless eyes, indicating, she later found out, a strong internet connection. There was something about the robot that made her feel uncomfortable, a little creeped-out.

When the men finished talking, they took questions from the floor, their enthused faces so slick in the harsh glare of the strip-lights above that Marcie wondered if HouseBOT had polished them too. The enquiries came thick and fast, like a hail of stones. Could she think? Talk? How much did she cost? Did she need sleep? Don had elbowed his way to the front of the crowd, and asked how many had been made. This was the prototype, the men explained, but there were a thousand more ready for sale, all with a Siri-like voice interface. No set-up required.

Marcie ended up taking the Metro home by herself as Don stayed behind to find out about the zero-per-cent financing plan the company was offering.

***

A week after Don had first mentioned acquiring HouseBOT, Marcie left work early and retrieved her car from the automated garage, waiting just a few minutes while the system shuffled SUVs like a vending machine slings snacks. She dropped the kids at judo, then went home and was surprised to find Jovilyn doing the ironing with teary eyes.

"God, what's happened?" she asked, flinging her bag onto the stairs. Don wouldn't have, would he? He surely hadn't let her go, when she'd expressly told him not to. She'd kill him if he had. The warm smell of ironing and sound of birdsong coming through the open window struck Marcie as incongruous in the presence of Jovilyn's obvious distress.

"It's my Ma," she sobbed. "She's in hospital, with a suspected stroke." Jovilyn ran the iron over a t-shirt a little too forcefully, and steam clouded up from the bright red material.

"Come and sit down," instructed Marcie gently. "Leave the ironing." She led her to the sofa, and listened while Jovilyn told her about the urgent phone call from her panic-stricken sister in the Philippines, the hospital bill they would face, and her useless, drunk father. Jovilyn shuddered, covering her eyes with her hands, and wailed, "I need to get home. I need to be there when she gets out of hospital to help her recover."

Marcie knew immediately that they'd do the right thing – pay the airfare *and* probably contribute to the medical expenses too – even as a disappointed hole began to form inside her stomach, an empty, nervous space that wondered what the hell she'd do without Jovilyn. She knew instantly, too, what Don would say.

She was right. She was always right when it came to predicting her husband. That evening, he agreed not only to fund Jovilyn's trip home but also to wire money to her family. When their housemaid was out of earshot talking to her sister on Skype, he announced they'd get HouseBOT in as a replacement.

"We've got no idea when – or if – Jovilyn will return," he reasoned. "There's an option to do a three-month trial before committing." His eyebrows danced, and Marcie threw her hands into the air, out of options.

***

HouseBOT arrived on a relatively cool day for Dubai. Streaky clouds dusted the sky and a slight breeze rustled the bougainvillea billowing over the rail in the front garden. Marcie watched from the kitchen window as HouseBOT was unloaded from the back of a truck. Don and the kids were already outside. Two men carried her in carefully, and placed her in the middle of the lounge. Then they all stood around her in a circle, waiting to see what her first move would be.

She waved, a slow mechanical gesture that sent the children into fits of giggles, their eyes too big for their lids. The men handed Don an instruction manual thicker than the Bible and he immediately started leafing through it, devouring it as though consumed with hunger.

Marcie forced a smile. "It is possible to turn her off, isn't it?" she asked, filled with trepidation at the sight of HouseBOT striding on flat feet to the window. The children followed her, and gasped as she rubbed at a smear on the glass with the pads on her metallic silver fingers. She dropped her robotic arm back to her side, and became motionless again, silent apart from a continuous, low whirring noise from deep inside her torso.

Reassured that it was possible to unplug her, Marcie turned her attention to the stream of friends and neighbours knocking at the door, all curious to meet the family's new robot help. With HouseBOT's assistance, she served cakes and sandwiches to their visitors, and the afternoon took on a party atmosphere, presided over by Don, whose face glowed red with pride. He waxed lyrical to anyone who would listen about HouseBOT's artificial intelligence, her ability to go up stairs, and the way she was programmed to achieve maximum efficiency at all times.

The last of their guests left as the sun set in a pool of crimson and gold, and Marcie went into the kitchen to clear up. HouseBOT had beaten her to it. She was standing at the open dishwasher, her rigid spine straight, as if she had an ironing board at her back. Marcie nervously watched as she stooped to stack the dirty plates, repeating the quick movements in a rhythm more attuned to a manufacturing line.

A dish smashed against the floor. Marcie cringed as the cracked pieces shot out in all directions.

"Not to worry," she said briskly, bending over to pick up the larger shards. HouseBOT didn't react. The robot merely moved to the sink and turned the tap on too hard to wash the iron skillet and wooden handled spatula. Water sprayed upwards onto the window, and droplets traced down the glass leaving mottled tracks.

When HouseBOT spoke, in a high, tinny, monotone voice, Marcie nearly jumped out of her skin.

"Washing-up liquid no good … Corrosive."

Marcie stared at her new employee, dumbstruck. "Must change brand," bleeped HouseBOT, shaking her head back and forth like a puppet on strings.

Marcie's hand flew to her throat in astonishment as the computerised voice continued, explaining which cleaning fluids she needed to protect her sensitive alloys. The familiar, uneasy feeling ambushed Marcie again. She really didn't want to share her home with this strange, bossy machine.

That night, a sense that there was a stranger in the house, an intruder, meant Marcie hardly slept. She was awoken early by the sound of the vacuum cleaner, loud and roaring outside their room. She sat up, wondering how on earth Don was able to sleep through such a noisy disturbance. He stirred, letting out a gaspy snore, and opened his eyes slowly. She squinted at the digital display on the clock radio she kept tuned to her favourite Dubai station. 6:02am. Ridiculously early. The grey light of dawn was only just creeping round the curtains.

Climbing out of bed, her eyes gritty with exhaustion, she slid her feet into her slippers and marched out of the bedroom.

All the lights were on in the landing, and she blinked as her vision adjusted. Hoover marks on the Persian rug glared up at her. The children appeared at their doors, bleary-eyed. HouseBOT was pointing the nozzle upwards, at a ninety-degree angle, about to run the vacuum over a wall-hanging.

"Stop," Marcie cried over the din. "You don't need to hoover that." But HouseBOT carried on, and she watched in dismay as a panel of material was sucked away from the wall in a bunch.

"For goodness sake," snapped Marcie, walking to the plug to cut the power. Silence fell, and her shoulders dropped. They clenched again as she asked HouseBOT if she knew what time it was. "Go back to bed everyone," she instructed, rubbing her palm over her forehead and knowing she might as well get up.

***

Over the next few weeks, there was a maelstrom of domestic mishaps as HouseBOT threw all the coloured laundry in with the whites, broke glasses, spilt disinfectant and dug up flowers instead of weeds in the garden.

Marcie had never done so much cleaning herself. She polished surfaces, pushed the Hoover around, dusted furniture, wiped windows. The children helped when they weren't at school, and slowly but surely HouseBOT began to up her game. It was as though she was watching and learning, copying the way chores were done. She stopped making silly mistakes and became quite proficient, even dependable.

One morning before work, Marcie realised that they'd settled into a routine, in which she could leave for the office knowing everything would be ship-shape by the time she got home. She'd even grown quite fond of HouseBOT. That night she'd dreamt HouseBOT had rusted after getting caught by the sprinklers outside, and was relieved to awaken and find her shelling peas in the kitchen, her metal frame as shiny and spot-free as ever, red light blinking behind her eyes like a beacon.

***

While driving to pick up the kids, the sky turned in a matter of seconds from being clear, blue and sunny to the midst of a sandstorm. The shamal billowed and swirled, flinging sand everywhere, and filled the sky with a thick, fog-like dust. It settled in like slow blindness, sucking the colour from the sun and the cars on the road. The highway became hazardous and Marcie was glad to get home safely with the children. Just the short walk from the car into school and back had left itchy sand in her scalp, ears and mouth.

For the rest of the afternoon, the wind bent the trees like twigs. The remaining daylight was tinged with yellow and stretched long and thin as the shamal continued to whip up a storm. Marcie sat down at her computer to finish off some work and noticed a strip of sand on her desk, under the closed window; the tiny, light, crystalline particles in stark contrast to the shiny, black lacquer surface.

She blew the grains away and wiped her desk with a tissue, knowing that downstairs far more sand would be pouring into the house through gaps under doors and window-frames. It was when sandstorms blew in that she was reminded how poorly sealed their villa was. The messy, ultra fine dust particles always found their way in somehow.

She glanced out the window and sneezed. She could smell dust. Everything, from the garden furniture to the paving stones and plants, was coated in a bleak, greyish brown veil as though a nuclear bomb had dropped. The cleanup would take hours. Thank goodness HouseBOT was on the case, thanklessly sweeping away the sand piled up on the balcony before it was lashed with another bucket-load of the stuff.

As spring brought more sandstorms and Marcie's hours at work were extended, she began depending on HouseBOT more than ever.

"So what do you think? Shall we make her permanent?" asked Don.

She paused before answering. Jovilyn had asked for more time in the Philippines; her mother was still recovering, and she was afraid to leave her in case she relapsed. Marcie suspected Jovilyn might have got back with her husband. "Alright," she replied, wringing her hands. "Sign the contract."

***

"Mum!" cried Marcie's older child. "Where's my PE kit?" Marcie came down the stairs to direct the getting-out-of-the house debacle, and was stopped in her tracks by a piece of paper thrust in her face. "Mum, I need your permission for the field trip," grumbled her youngest. She found a pen and scrawled a spidery signature on the slip then reached for her purse.

The morning's chaos seemed worse than normal, and she hadn't even looked through their school bags yet for fear of opening a Pandora's box of not-done homework, crumpled artwork and notes about missing library books. She felt a little squiffy after a late night at Don's annual work dinner at the Kempinski, and he'd left early to visit a client in Abu Dhabi, muttering as he went that he wished they'd hurry up and open the Hyperloop. Dubai to Abu Dhabi in under 15 minutes, it "will happen", he was fond of saying to anyone who'd listen.

"Where's HouseBOT?" Marcie asked the children, seeing that she wasn't in the kitchen as usual making toast.

"Come and have a look," said her youngest and led her into the lounge. HouseBOT was lying on the sofa, her fake limbs sprawled over the seat, head twisted at an angle that would have been uncomfortable for humans.

"Is she okay?" gasped Marcie, shocked by the glimpse of twisted tubes under her trunk. "Where's the red light? Oh God, what's happened?"

She put her hand on HouseBOT's hard forehead, and the robot whirred to life, the red beam protruding out again from her bulbous eyes and her parts clunking back into place. She rose quickly and, without speaking, left the room. Marcie instantly knew something wasn't right.

She found HouseBOT in the same position the following morning, and laid out on a garden lounger when she got home from work that afternoon. After dinner, she talked to Don about it. "It's really strange," she said, "HouseBOT has got so clever at knowing how to do things, sorting, organising, putting everything in the right place. But it's like she's suddenly got lazy and doesn't want to work anymore."

Don looked puzzled. He'd keep an eye on it, he said.

The next day, when Marcie got home from the supermarket the house hadn't even been tidied. The breakfast bowls were still in the sink, clothes flowed unfolded from the laundry basket, and there were chess pieces strewn all over the lounge. Her children had taken a passing interest in chess a while ago, and then forgotten all about it, so she was surprised to see they'd discovered the game again. Could they not at least tidy it away, she raged to herself as she picked up a red sandalwood king lying under the coffee table.

She went to unpack the groceries and, once finished, began the washing up, glancing out the window every now and then looking for HouseBOT. The sun was high in the sky and glared off the solar panels on the rooftop opposite, lighting them up like a tanning salon. HouseBOT was nowhere to be seen.

When the kids traipsed in from a neighbour's house, she demanded to know why they hadn't cleared up their chess game. Blank faces glowered back at her. "Wasn't us, Mum," they claimed indignantly.

"Has anyone seen HouseBOT?" she asked. The children shook their heads.

HouseBOT finally showed up just before dinner, and said she'd been walking round the neighbourhood, lost after taking a wrong turn on the way back from the supermarket. Trying to throw off the thought that their robot cleaner was acting like a third child, Marcie nodded and silently served the lasagna.

Matters didn't get any better over the following week. Some of HouseBOT's strange behaviour could be passed off as amusing, like when Marcie found her trying on the children's clothes and pivoting round in front of the mirror. But other things, like leaving the gas on, were inexcusable. Marcie ran round the house opening the windows, trying to get rid of the smell of rotten eggs, her face alight with rage. Livid, she called Don at work. "HouseBOT has to go," she told him. "She could have killed us all this afternoon."

"Perhaps you're working her too hard," suggested Don. "If you ease up on her a bit, things might go back to normal."

Marcie slammed the phone down, blinking furiously to stem the hot tears scalding her eyes. When Don got home, she threatened to leave if he didn't arrange for HouseBOT to be returned to the manufacturer. She was done with robot help. She wanted to throw the over-long, tediously boring instruction manual at her husband's technology-obsessed head.

The truck pulled up the next afternoon, and Marcie breathed a sigh of relief at having their house to themselves again. Getting their money back wasn't going to be easy, and she'd have to cut her work hours down somehow, but she wanted no part of Don's experiment anymore. She should have trusted her instincts when she'd first seen HouseBOT at the Expo. Pulling her phone out, she sent Jovilyn a message to ask if she was ready to come back. The answer, to Marcie's joy, was a resounding yes.

Marcie was outside hanging the laundry out when she saw the chequered pattern on the paving stones. Someone had used black and white chalks to create a chessboard, a complete, perfectly proportioned grid of squares. She walked over to it and peered at the ground, remembering the kids' denial at leaving their chess pieces scattered all over the lounge floor. She scuffed at a white square with her foot, smudging the outline so it bled into the grouting. Had HouseBOT taken up chess? Could that explain why she'd become so lax at her job?

Her suspicions were confirmed that evening after Don got off the phone with the head roboticist. Shaking his head with disbelief, he told Marcie what their analysis of the downloads from HouseBOT's internal hard drive had shown.

"She spent the last month playing chess – day and night," Don said incredulously. She'd become a grandmaster, a much-feared opponent who'd signed up for an international tournament in Moscow and was competing with the creme de la creme of the chess world. HouseBOT didn't need a computer to play – her internal internet connection hooked her straight up to the games, which could go on for hours. When the house was empty and she wasn't playing competitively, she practised on the family's chessboard and the chalkboard outside, moving the pieces around, searching for combinations, and replaying games and positions shown to her by world champion Magnus Carlsen.

Marcie remembered the red beam that shone behind her eyes – an indecipherable pulse that hid just how much artificial intelligence she was gaining – and smiled, half admiring, half a little disturbed at where this intellect could lead. Just how clever could these machines become?

"It's no wonder her 'mind'," said Don, using two fingers on each hand to draw air quotes, "wasn't on the job." He looked sheepish for a moment. "There was something I wanted to talk to you about, that might make up for losing HouseBOT."

"What do you mean?" Marcie swallowed hard. "Jovilyn will be back in two weeks' time."

"Just hear me out. I've been in contact with this guy who's offering me a great deal. Do you remember seeing those driverless cars at the Expo?"

The Pearl Divers
May 1949

Amir peered into the seawater, past the ripples lapping against the boat's wooden frame and squinted into the deep blue below. A shadow caught his eye, a murky flickering with indistinct edges at least fifteen feet down, but it was gone before the smudge became a man. Swallowed by a wave that rolled and licked.

The boat rocked and Amir felt a well of pride rising up in his chest. Although just a glimpse, he knew the dark shape was his father, Nadim, scouring the seabed for oysters with a knife. No-one on the eighteen-man Emirati crew, not even his uncle, could hold their breath underwater for as long as his *Baba*.

The divers worked without breathing apparatus, and Amir was counting how many seconds his father had been submerged for, a silent, rhythmic ticking in his head that eased the monotony on board and told him when to expect the tug on the rope.

His warm glow of admiration was quickly dissolved by the sound of the *Nakhuda's* (captain's) voice. "Get back on deck, boy," he shouted. The steady drum in Amir's mind stopped abruptly and he nearly lost count.

Springing away from the low timber rail, he sat down, crossing his skinny, brown legs. The floorboards were drenched and moisture crept up the already-soggy fabric of his shorts, leaving a dark, wet ring. His thin chest was bare, as were his blistered feet. The breeze-blown air tasted salty and his hands were sore from tugging at the rope.

Their sailing dhow was anchored in a slight chop and Amir tightened his grip on the thick, frayed cord that snaked into the sea. He watched as his uncle, Hosni, stepped into a loop of rope attached to a rock, twisted it around his leg and jumped into the water, sinking quickly to the bottom. A basket, attached to a second rope, plunged to the seabed with him.

177-178-179. Amir waited and counted. *Baba should be ready to surface by now. Where is he?*

After three minutes, Amir always started to feel uneasy, aware that his father's empty lungs must be about to burst. He also knew there were sharks down there. Immediately, like a guillotine coming down, he stopped that thought dead.

It was only an hour after sunrise, and the morning light speared his eyes as it angled into the boat, shining brilliantly on the single white sail flapping in the light wind and catching the chrome perfection of the *Nakhuda's* very simple compass. The captain mostly navigated by the stars, and the crew all trusted his knowledge of the pearl banks, which were generally some distance from the coast.

182-183-184. No-one else was alarmed, but then Amir was the only person who kept track of the seconds. *185-186-187 … 192.* He sprung to his feet, and stared without blinking into the sea. The sky, a blank, pale watery blue, drew in around him.

Come on Baba. Pull. Time to come up.

The tug came just as Amir was about to alert his *Seib* (main puller). Suddenly, the *Seib* was hauling in fast, hand over hand. Amir, a half puller, pulled from behind. It still took a while before they saw any sign of Nadim, deep below. The shadow became a blurred outline, and at last his father broke water. His basket first, filled to the brim with oysters, then his weather-beaten face with a hand flung up to shield his bloodshot eyes from the bright sun. He gasped for air and shook his head, then blew once, twice, like a whale.

Amir grinned at his father as he floated in the water. Nadim's cracked lips curved upwards in a smile that spread to his water-tired eyes. Father and son shared a moment.

"203 seconds!" said Amir over the sound of the shells being poured into a large pan. "A record," he mouthed. It was his father's best dive ever, and the longest by far that day – by the end of which Nadim, Hosni and the rest of the men had completed nearly 50 dives each, breaking only for prayers, coffee and a short rest at midday.

That night, as the deck swayed under them and the stars arched high above the dhow, the crew ate a meal of fish and rice, before gathering in a circle around the pile of oyster shells collected that day. They were opened under the watchful eye of the captain, who recorded any particularly big pearls which could be sold individually. Amir sat between his father and uncle, eagerly watching, hoping for a good haul. He was well aware that the industry that had fed his family for generations was being decimated by cheaper, artificially produced Japanese pearls. Amir knew their livelihood was under threat.

His family, and everyone on board, was in debt to the *Nakhuda*, who each season handed out advances to the divers so they could provide for their wives and children on shore. Last year, profits had been so low that the divers' debt had been carried over, making the amount owed this season even more crippling. Amir had overheard his father and uncle saying they wouldn't be free from debt in this lifetime.

Fresh tension erupted that evening as an argument broke out between Hosni and a fellow diver over who had found the biggest pearl. His father led Amir away from the fracas, and they settled down on the crowded deck for the night, availing themselves of any cooling sea breezes.

"Baba," whispered Amir.

"What is it?" his father replied.

"When can I dive?"

"Soon son. Soon. Go to sleep."

The next day, diving commenced after a breakfast of coffee and dates. Amir pulled in the stifling heat until it seemed his arms might pop out of their sockets. He pulled until the sun began its slow ascent into the Western sky, and kept going until mid-afternoon, when his sore shoulders finally got a break. He was fiddling with a discarded nose clip made from turtle shell when a shadow in the shape of a large man blocked the light like a dark, thundery cloud. He looked up, at the Nakhuda's scowling eyebrows. Whenever he frowned, the whites of his eyes disappeared. His mood must be black again. "Hey, you," barked the captain.

Yes, Sir," Amir responded, automatically. He let the clip fall from his fingers and it dropped onto the deck with a clunk.

"The cook's sick. I need you in the galley – now." The captain walked off without another word.

Amir jumped up and went to the tiny, enclosed kitchen below deck, wondering what had happened to his friend, a ten-year-old apprentice, just like him. The smell from the vegetable broth bubbling on the stove tickled his nose and he let out a sigh. He wanted to be a diver more than anything. Just like his *Baba* and uncle, and their father before them. Amir was tired of being told he was too young, that diving was too dangerous, the risk of drowning or damaged eardrums too high. With two arduous pearling seasons under his belt, he didn't see why he should have to wait any longer.

He was sure that if he was allowed to enter the blue underworld to search for pearls, he'd find the elusive pink pearl, the most precious of a range of colours, or, if he was really lucky, perhaps a black pearl. So lustrous and captivating that even the most daring divers in their corner of the ocean would know his name by heart.

***

The dhow was visited the next morning by the local merchants who arrived at the pearl banks from time to time with sieves, scales and magnifying glasses. They divided the haul up by size and quality. Amir's father had explained the process: the pearls were stored in rainwater to remove the greenish tinge, then wrapped in scarlet cloth.

Voices were raised as a price – much lower than hoped – was agreed in front of the two-thirds of the crew required to be present to witness the sale.

As the traders receded, another angry argument began on board. Amir knew his uncle had a fiery temperament, but had never seen him so riled up. Hosni's face turned almost as crimson as the red kerchiefs the pearls were sold in. "They're robbing us," he yelled.

The *Nakhuda* told him to beat it. The price was fair given the market conditions.

"No," cried Hosni. "We need modern equipment if we're to compete."

"Deep-sea diving suits for a start," chipped in another resentful voice.

The captain laughed, a thin and contemptuous sound. "Britain and the ruling families are resistant to new ways of working. You don't need me to tell you that."

"Why?" spat Hosni, his fists clenched around his temper. Nadim appeared by his brother's side and laid a hand on his shoulder. Hosni shrugged it off.

The captain puffed out a breath and clicked his tongue over misaligned, yellow front teeth. "They fear an uprise–"

"So they're prepared to let us die out here?" Hosni cut in. "And then what? Our families starve?"

Crouched on the deck, Amir wondered if he was about to witness a fight.

"Modernisation won't happen – artificial aids come with great risks," the captain continued. "Now get back to work." He strode off, leaving the men huddled together in bitter silence.

Later, when Hosni had calmed down, he told Amir and Nadim what else was troubling him. "Our *Nakhuda* is holding back pearls to sell independently," he said in a tight, betrayed voice. He'd seen the *Nakhuda* pocket a pearl. "There's no life left in this industry ... we're all doomed," he moaned, flattening his hair with thick, rough hands, eyes glassy in the moonlight. Amir saw his chance.

"*Baba*, let me dive," he pleaded. "You've always said I'm your lucky son. Please – I'm ready to dive." A bead of sweat crept from his father's hairline.

"I've waited so long. You've already taught me everything I need to know." He realised his voice had risen. His heartbeat quickened.

A stare passed between them, and then Nadim finally relented. "Okay, tomorrow."

"Thank you *Baba*," said Amir, and punched the air.

***

The preparations for Amir's dive were carried out quietly, just after sunrise. His father and uncle coated his skin in oil, plugged his ears with cotton wool, and placed leather sheaths over his fingers and toes to protect against razor-sharp rocks. Hosni hung a rope basket around his neck, then tucked a knife into his belt. It gleamed as it caught the light.

"Still want to dive?" Nadim asked, his gaze unblinking in the sunshine.

"Yes," said Amir, nodding. He flexed his thin, muscular arms, trying to free the adrenalin. *At last.* This was it. At that moment, the boy became a man. An oyster hunter. He puffed out his bare chest as he grew in stature, and felt himself grow taller. His mother's proud face flashed into his mind.

Amir stood still as his father placed a clip over his nose, pinching his nostrils together. "Good luck," said Nadim, and patted him on the shoulder. Hosni, smiling broadly, gave him a salute. Clutching his basket by the rim and holding a heavy stone tied with a rope, Amir moved to the side of the boat.

He took in a deep breath, filling his lungs to capacity, and jumped. Down he went, down, down, an arrow piercing its target. After the initial rush of water, an eerie, silent stillness pulled at his limbs. He opened his eyes and had the sense he'd entered another world, without edges or daylight. Silt and dust floated upwards as he plummeted deeper, through different shades of blue and a shoal of fish that shimmered away like quick silver.

The water was warm at first but grew chillier as the ocean's aquamarine colour gave way to cobalt and then a murky, dark indigo that pressed into him. His foot touched the bottom with a jolt and sand clouded up, mixing with the flotsam and jetsam suspended all around him. The pressure felt different and he equalised his ears, as he'd been taught. A poof sound, followed by a sensation of fullness in his eardrums. A stream of tiny bubbles escaped his lips.

Amir worked fast, scraping oysters off rocks with his knife and storing them in his neck-basket. "Look for the ugliest you can find," his father had told him, and so he searched for shells with holes, wide hinges and barnacles clamped to the outside.

When his lungs could take no more, he tugged on the line and was hauled up to the surface. He felt euphoric as he hit air, drawing in one, two, three sharp breaths, gulping, coughing. He held his basket up like a trophy. Through watery eyes, he saw the pinched, worried expression on his father's face dissolve into a proud, beaming smile.

Amir's shells were kept to one side while he resumed his pulling duties for the rest of the day. Nadim was anxious he shouldn't dive again until tomorrow, to minimise side effects such as nausea and aches.

His shells were cut open as the sun slid under the horizon, turning the sky a rich, pinky orange. The water was mirror still. Out of 23 shells, there was only one pearl, glistening but tiny. As smooth and round as a miniature glass marble, but worth very little.

"Nice work," said his father, sensing his disappointment. "From 100 oysters, you can expect just one pearl – did I not tell you that, son?"

Amir nodded, silently vowing to hold his breath for longer the next day.

***

Amir became an accomplished diver before the season was out, his crowning glory being a pearl the size of a chickpea that fetched a decent price. One evening, when the crew was busy mending baskets, Amir saw the *Nakhuda* swallow a pearl; he recoiled with disgust at the thought of the captain retrieving the stolen pearl. They didn't dare try to prove that the *Nakhuda* was selling precious finds on the side, though, and remained loyal, so sizeable was their family's debt to him.

Between seasons, Amir, Nadim and Hosni kept busy on land, tending date gardens and herding camels. When April rolled around, Amir's mother begged them not to go pearling. She'd heard about jobs in Kuwait, where oil had blasted through a wellhead under such pressure and in such quantity that the gusher couldn't be contained. The first tankers had left Kuwait, loaded with thick, black, treacle-like crude. She showed Nadim the job ad, and suggested Amir join him as soon as he was old enough. "It's going to change everything," she said boldly.

Nadim shrugged. "Pearling's what I know," he said and gave a short, sharp shake of his head. He wasn't convinced. He was a fisherman at heart, a man of the sea.

Amir felt his mother's arms clasping him, holding him close, so tight she squeezed the air from his lungs. "Then let Amir stay behind? I can't sleep for worrying."

It had been easier on her nerves, she said, when she didn't know he was plunging into the Gulf's sweet, salty water and scouring the seabed for pearls. Dive five times, rest, repeat; chanting to ease the rigorous tasks on board.

"Mama, I have to go with *Baba*," said Amir quietly, and the next day, he was on the dhow as it departed with all the other boats in a picturesque swoop of sail.

As it turned out, his mother was losing sleep over the wrong person. Hosni died that trip. The cause was unclear. The death certificate stated drowning, but with such desperate poverty affecting their sea shanty town there was a rumour among the crew that he had taken his own life. Hosni was given a sea burial; with suicide prohibited in Islam, Amir was forbidden from ever talking about the circumstances surrounding his uncle's death.

Four months and ten days after setting sail, their dhow returned to the port. Despite their heavy hearts over losing Hosni, the joy of coming home was more precious than all the pearls they'd collected and sold.

Amir's mother wasted no time. "It's begun," she said, pinning her husband with shrewd eyes.

"What?"

"Large-scale oil production."

They were sitting at the table and she pushed a newspaper over the wooden surface. "Look," she said, pointing a calloused finger at the black-and-white print of the Jobs section.

Amir watched with baited breath as his father stared at the text, chewing his moustache, struggling to read the words.

Nadim looked up. Then he fished out a red silk kerchief from his pocket and untied a knot in the fabric to reveal a shiny pearl. Amir heard a gasp, his mother's. At her eyes-wide-open reaction, Nadim took her hand and said he'd think about applying. "I carry this for luck," he told his wife, winking broadly at her, "but if work takes me to Kuwait then I want you to have it, for safekeeping."

Cellmates

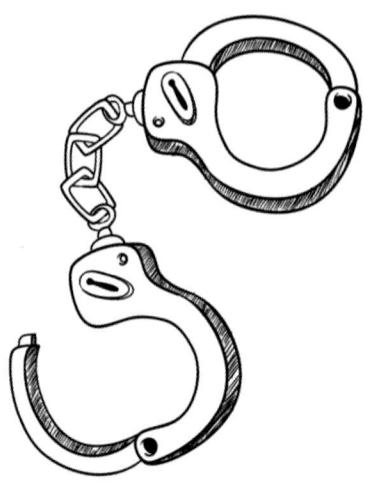

Mandi cradled her throbbing head in her hands. A hangover was gathering strength behind her eyes like an oncoming storm. A bad one, made worse by zero sleep. Through the gaps between her fingers she could see her cellmate, sitting cross-legged on the bug-infested mattress, a grey, prison-issue blanket tangled around her slim ankles.

Her companion, Camila, was thin and beautiful, and wore a canary yellow sundress. Jaeger, at a guess. Sleeveless, low-cut and tied at her waist with a gold cord, the floaty chiffon fabric was as crumpled as old parchment paper but still looked stunning and expensive against her cinnamon skin. A black-and-white rose tattoo covered the top of her left arm.

Hostility bristled between the two women, ebbing and flowing around them like an invisible force-field. They mostly avoided eye contact, which was just as well as when they did lock eyes, Mandi felt as though she was being speared. She tried to sleep, only to snap wide awake again at the sound of a hoarse, angry voice.

"Dis nightmare is all your fault."

Camila was from Peru and spat the words out like a Siamese cat trying to cough up a hairball. Without warning, she began to retch violently, her small frame racked by the intensity of her heaving.

Mandi grabbed the pan propped up against the brick wall, and shoved it under Camila's chin – just in time. She pulled a tissue from her pocket to cover her own mouth and nose. The piss-sour stench in the windowless cell was already bad enough; it had hit them when the policemen locked them inside at two in the morning. Five sleepless hours later, it smelt as strong as when they'd first arrived, handcuffed and frightened.

Holding her breath, Mandi swiped the noxious pan away and placed it by the thick, steel door. Swallowing her own sick feeling, she tried to conjure up a different olfactory sense. Peppermint, chewing gum, or Trent's soapy, frisky smell. He gave off the kind of scent – alluring and manly with a top note of citrus – that seemed to intensify whenever things heated up between them. Mandi wondered how he was faring in his cell, whether he'd been allowed to make a phone call or take a shower. Whether he was thinking about her or glamour-puss Camila.

The dank, cramped space they were sharing was so tiny the two filthy mattresses had been pushed right up together to leave room for a single plastic chair. A bare, electric bulb provided the only light. They'd been given clean sheets by a warden who looked like a man but could have been a woman, and had tried not to think about where the stains on the mattresses had come from.

"Do you want some water?" Mandi asked.
Camila nodded.
Mandi reached for the water bottle under the chair, passed it over and watched as Camila tilted her head back and took several large gulps, swallowing without a breath. Water spilled from the corners of her lips.

Camila wiped her mouth with the back of her hand. Without her sparkling rock of a diamond ring, her fingers looked naked. As did her wrist. Last night it had been decorated with a fancy gold watch, a present from Trent. They'd both stuffed their valuables in their bras when they'd realised how much trouble they were in. Just after they were stripped of their phones, handbags and high heels. They'd even had to throw their tampons away.

As Camila stiffened, elongating her spine until she was as straight-backed as a meerkat, Mandi steeled herself to face another tirade. Camila's mouth twisted and her lips punched out the words Mandi knew she deserved. "Tell me again, exactly what did you think you were going to achieve by sleeping with him?" Her dark eyes flashed. "You knew we were meant to be getting married this summer. I don't know what he saw in a little tart like you anyway."

Mandi lowered her head. "How many times do you want me to say sorry? I regret it, okay." She felt a guilty flush creep up from beneath her pink and cream satin dress.

"Of course you regret it. Look where we are!" Camila gesticulated wildly with one arm, and Mandi noticed the small, skin-coloured oval plaster on the inside of her elbow. Hers had fallen off within minutes of the blood test carried out by an official who'd held her arm down and jabbed her with a sharp needle. She recalled the line of syringes on a tray beside him and shuddered.

"We're locked up, at Bur Dubai police station," Camila continued, her voice rising. She emphasised the name of the infamous police cells by sounding each syllable. "We could go to PRISON. We've signed unintelligible papers written in Arabic. Our passports are being held. This is serious shit Mandi. They're probably going to make an example out of us. Send a warning to all the other drunk Brits, just like you, who come to Dubai and don't abide by the law."

"You shouldn't have gone nuts," Mandi shot back, defensively. "You went crazy. If you hadn't acted like such a mad woman, we wouldn't be in this hellhole now."

Camila gave a derisory snort. "Oh yeah! We should have all sat on the bed and talked about it, should we?" She rolled her eyes. "You were completely naked. *Bitch!*"

Mandi didn't reply, and they lapsed into another dreadful silence.

If she could have paced the cell, she would have done, but there wasn't room. There wasn't enough space to swing a cat. She hugged her knees to her chest, shoulders sagging, back aching from lying for hours on the saggy mattress. She shifted position and looked down at her hands. Two of her scarlet lacquered nails were chewed short, bitten anxiously to the quick. She needed a wash, a long, hot shower, so badly, and really wanted to clean her teeth to get rid of the taste of tequila.

Camila sank back on the mattress and groaned. "When – if – we get out of here, we could be deported." She sniffed and wiped away a tear. Mandi gave her a tissue and she took it without speaking. Camila dabbed at her face, sat up, and then before Mandi really knew what was happening, she crossed her legs, raised her hands above her head and clapped them together as though in prayer. Was she seriously doing yoga? In a prison cell, of all places.

With nowhere else to look, Mandi's gaze shifted to the blank wall in front of her. The mustard-coloured paint was peeling off like flecks of dried skin. What the hell was she going to tell her boss? For her first proper job, she'd been making good commission selling properties on the Palm. *What will mum say? Will she even visit me if I end up in prison?* That new boyfriend of hers would have to pay for her to fly out – if he even let her come. Mandi wasn't sure he would.

Ten minutes and four yoga poses later, Camila sat in the lotus position with her hands on her knees.

"Feel better?" Mandi asked.

"Yes – you should try it. Trent loves all the moves I can throw in bed. Can't get enough of them."

Their attention was diverted by the sound of the heavy door being unlocked from the other side. A slither of outside noise, a foreign-sounding shout, a radio blaring loud Arabic music, poured in though the gap. A bunch of keys jangled. The door swung open wider, and a police officer stepped in, holding a tray. He placed it on the chair. "Breakfast," he said, and left, taking the contaminated pan with him. The door locked with a click behind him.

Rubbery globs of congealed scrambled eggs stared up from two ugly brown plastic plates. The servings had already curled at the edges like old, yellowed wallpaper. A pile of flatbread lay in the middle of the tray, next to two plastic spoons. "All yours," hissed Camila.

Mandi shook her head. "Not hungry," she replied. "What time is it anyway?"

Camila reached into her bra and pulled out her gold watch. "Seven fifteen."

With no natural light, it could easily still be three in the morning. "I wonder what you have to do to get a cup of tea around here," joked Mandi.

Camila didn't laugh.

The police officer returned a few minutes later. "You can make phone calls – one each," he told them, as though offering them brownies. They quickly scrambled to their feet and followed him out of the cell. They were allowed to put their shoes back on to walk to the office, and were both eager to do so, despite the obvious impracticality of Mandi's four-inch Christian Louboutins. Their heels clacked against the hard floor as they walked along the corridor, turning right through a guarded swingdoor into another artificially lit passageway. They were underground, but thank God hadn't been handcuffed again. Mandi remembered very little about the direction they'd taken last night. She'd felt like a rabbit about to die, and didn't feel much better now.

A man, chained to a uniformed officer, passed them in the opposite direction, staring at their legs. His jaw dropped, and Mandi wondered what he was in for. Christ, he could be a rapist.

She knew there was no point both of them trying to call Trent, but who was she going to ring? It was the middle of the night in England, and she wasn't ready to tell her mum about her arrest yet. Her good friends in the UK wouldn't mind being woken up, but what could they do from so far away? She hadn't been in Dubai long enough to make any friendships that weren't totally fake. *Will any of my new mates even care?* An imagined pain like a latticework of barbed wire spread across her chest. She decided to call a lawyer and in a trembly voice asked the police officer if he knew any good ones. The kind that could get her off a charge of immoral conduct in an unforgiving Dubai court governed by sharia law.

***

Mandi was ushered to a meeting room a little after eleven. Her lawyer sat at a table waiting for her, dressed in a grey suit, with brown, combed-over hair and deepset eyes that regarded her shrewdly. He stood when she entered and they shook hands, his dry palms clasping hers firmly. "Eliot Batholew-Higgins," he said. "Nice to meet you."

A leather-bound diary lay on the desk in front of him, and he wrote a few notes with a fountain pen as they talked. "So was this the first time you'd met Trent?" he asked, keeping his gaze level.

Mandi cleared her throat. "Erm, no. It wasn't. We'd seen each other a few times before."

"And Camila didn't know about this?"

"No."

"Where did you think she was last night?"

"Trent said she was away on a work trip."

"But she let herself back into the apartment, with her own key?"

"She did. That's when it all went wrong."

Mandi cast her mind back to how the disastrous evening had unfolded. She'd had no reason not to believe Trent when he'd said his girlfriend was gone. He did something in sales and could be very persuasive. She'd always fallen for his patter, ever since she'd shown him round a luxury apartment on the trunk of the Palm Jumeriah. Blessed with a charismatic smile, and a game-for-anything expression, Trent had charmed her right from the start.

She'd known last night would end in steamy sex from the moment he'd picked her up in his Lamborghini. He'd teamed a pair of dark denim jeans with a black T-shirt layered with a baseball-style jacket featuring numerous zips. While the elegant cuts of his business suits accentuated his toned body, he looked even better, even sexier, in casual clothes. On his feet he wore caramel-toned brogues.

After cocktails at At.mosphere, on floor 122 of the Burj Khalifa, they'd taken a taxi back to his apartment in Dubai Marina and carried on drinking. One thing led to another, and … well, there was no way she was telling the lawyer all about *that*.

The first hint they were being watched came when the main bedroom light was suddenly flicked on. The shock was like a camera flash going off.

She'd rolled off Trent and pulled the duvet up around her bare breasts. She remembered her nipples still being hard and fully erect.

Camila had jutted her chin, sniffing the smell of sex in the air like a dog might do. She marched over and yanked the comforter off, shouting over the sound of Trent pleading with her that he could explain. *Pah!* Camila had reeked of alcohol.

Mandi felt her face grow hot as she explained all this to the lawyer, sparing him the lurid details. He merely listened, nodding impassively.

Her hand instinctively rose to her cheek as she recalled Camila slapping her. "She hit me," Mandi told the lawyer. "Hard. Seriously, she was demented. Her eyes were weird – manic."

"Had she taken drugs?"

Mandi shrugged. "Dunno. But she was scaring me, and that's when I started screaming too."

"What was Trent doing at this point?"

"Still trying to do up his jeans."

"How long did the disturbance go on for?"

"Not that long. The police must have been nearby."

"Someone called them?"

"A downstairs neighbour."

She'd been pleased to see the policemen at first because Camila had just thrown a vase at Trent's head, narrowly missing. It smashed against the wall and Mandi wasn't sure what she would do next. Mandi had been trying to leave, but her clothes, bra and panties were littered around the apartment. If she'd been able to find her dress sooner, it might all have been okay. She'd be on her way to the pool now for a lazy Saturday afternoon rather than under arrest.

Silence had fallen as the police swooped in, but then Camila, her eyes red and bloodshot, pointed at Mandi and told the officers she'd just had illegal sex. They'd all been arrested for breaking strict Muslim morality laws.

"Right," said the lawyer after running through Mandi's limited options. "Let's get you out of here. I'll arrange for you to be released on bail."

***

A court appearance was scheduled for the next day. The trio turned up early, their faces as solemn as the imposing marble pillars flanking the courthouse. Trent's arm was draped over Camila's shoulders. He gave Mandi a half nod, before turning his attention back to his girlfriend as though no-one else bar her existed. Mandi noticed she wasn't wearing her engagement ring anymore.

The two women didn't speak. They were all ushered away to a formally furnished room, where Mandi's heart beat double time in her throat. Her stomach surged with nausea. The threat of prison had never felt so real.

In court, several charges were pressed: disturbing the peace, sex outside of marriage, and drinking at Trent's home without a licence. When the judge handed out month-long jail sentences to all three of them, Mandi let out an audible, anguished cry. The room started spinning, the colours diffusing into streaks and scattering, the floor swimming up to meet the windows, and she thought she might faint. Trent and Camila turned waxy-white, as though their faces had been dusted with flour.

Mandi called her mother as soon as she got home. The news was breaking in the press, and she didn't want her mum to find out from the *Daily Mail*. A journalist from the paper had already phoned, offering a substantial sum for her story, but on her lawyer's advice she didn't speak to him.

Her mum took it badly, as Mandi knew she would, and tearfully promised to try to fly out. Friends rang from the UK, so Mandi at least felt supported. But no-one could reverse the prison sentence, and a last-minute appeal was unsuccessful. Mandi would have to face the women's jail in the company of her worst enemy Camila.

***

The day she was due at the prison dawned bright, just like any other. Mandi left her apartment and told a surprised taxi driver where to go. The prison, a sprawling complex in the desert, had watch-towers and barbed wire on top of high, white walls. She was admitted and then issued with her uniform and bedding – two blankets and, because it was her 'lucky day', according to the warden, a pillow. It had all been washed at least.

She was searched by a woman who seemed to enjoy her job, and had to hand over her belongings. Her money went into a safe; leaving her three hundred dirhams a week to spend. There was a shop, selling a few groceries, cigarettes, headphone radios and batteries, and a travel agent (one-way tickets only). Pay phones were available for three hours every morning, and four hours in the afternoon.

Aside from the toilets, which were disgusting, stench-ridden holes in the ground where you had to squat, the thing that shocked Mandi the most was the very basic children's play area. Her hand flew to her mouth. "There's kids in here?"

The warden nodded. "Pregnant women who get sentenced have babies and raise them here."

"But that's ... " She struggled to find a word. "Awful," she finished, choking back tears.

The warden shrugged. "The kids are always fighting – over the few toys available. Pick up bad habits, they do."

Mandi and the warden walked the rest of the way to her dorm in silence. When they got there, Camilia was already lying on a bunk bed. She'd chosen the bottom bunk. Mandi glanced around, saw that all the other beds were taken, and climbed the iron ladder up to the un-made bed above Camila, who hadn't said a word. She lay down, stared at the ceiling, and realised that her stay was going to be terminally boring, especially if Camila kept up the radio silence. Which, given the animosity between them, wouldn't surprise her. There would be plenty of time to think about how to pay the bail money back and what to do about her career, now that she'd lost her job and had her visa cancelled.

The only positive Mandi could find was that, if the food was as rank as she expected, she might lose some weight.

Lunch was at eleven thirty am and consisted of rice and chicken slopped onto a plastic plate with a piece of lettuce and fruit for dessert. The food came on a metal tray and there was no cutlery, so it was hands only. Mandi was scraping her leftovers into a bucket when someone called her name. She looked up to see a chunky bulldog of a warden staring at her. "You're that English girl aren't you? Caught misbehaving … *Tut. Tut.* How's prison treating you, Melanie?"

"It's Mandi, actually." Shame spiraled through her for the umpteenth time. She'd been recognised a few times since the sentencing. Much of the international news coverage had been sympathetic, but in the comments section of the online local press – the space that hangs below articles like an unwanted growth – the vitriol had throbbed. *"Loutish expat behaviour has to stop*! *What did they expect? They're living in a country governed by Islam."* In the end, Mandi had banned herself from going online – it had got too distressing.

"So it's Mandi, eh?" said the warden, sizing her up and down. "Well, enjoy your stay."

Most of the inmates slept in the afternoon – with nothing much else to do, it passed the time. Having held on all morning, Mandi was forced to brave the toilet for the first time. She stood over the hole with one foot on either side, crouched down and, after initially losing the urge, managed to pee. The smell curdled in her nose. Terrified she might inadvertently touch the latrine, she stood without wiping. Bile rose in her throat. She'd never felt so alone in her life.

Lying on her bed, she attempted to read, but the more she stared at the words, the more their edges blurred. She eventually dozed off, only to come round to a waking nightmare as she remembered she was in jail. Digging deep inside herself to get a grip, she decided to try cajoling Camila into talking to her. She climbed down from her bunk and found Trent's fiance silently crying into her pillow.

"Hey, you okay?"

"Not really," she sniffed.

"Want to talk about it?"

"With you? … Hardly."

Mandi saw her chance. "Look, I really think we could help each other out over the next few weeks. Could we … perhaps be friends?"

Camila snorted. "I haven't forgiven you, if that's what you want."

"You don't have to – but maybe we could try to get on. Help each other through this."

"It's a bad idea. I can't stand you, remember. In fact, I HATE you. It's your fault my engagement is off." Camila turned her blotched face away, and another tear ran down her cheeks. "I'm not crying about Trent, or being in prison, in case you're wondering."

"Then what is it?"

"Did you know there are children in here?"

Mandi gave a grim nod.

"I just saw them playing – I can't believe they're locked up. There was a boy with the most beautiful, saddest eyes I've ever seen …" Camila faltered, her words tailing off as she dabbed at a tear. She was a woman who wore her emotions on her sleeve. She sniffed loudly again. "D'you think they've ever tasted the outside world?"

"I don't know," said Mandi quietly. She laid a hand on her room-mate's arm and Camila didn't shrug it off.

By lights out, hours later, Mandi had learned that the five other women sharing their dorm were from Iran, Ukraine,

Indonesia, Ethiopia and Nepal. None of them spoke English. They communicated with sign language. A warden told her two were prostitutes and the other three were migrant workers with no visa and big debts. Mandi hadn't smoked since her college days, but as she lay in bed, listening to loud snores, someone weeping and raised voices talking in a language she didn't understand outside, she wanted a cigarette so badly it was as though her life depended on it.

She heard a shuffle of sheets and the sound of feet being planted on the floor. Peering over the cold, metal rail of her bunk, she saw Camila's silhouette in the middle of the room, striking a perfect lotus pose. Her cellmate cut a beautiful figure in the dark, her white night-shirt stretched across pert breasts, stomach flat, arms and legs toned, and Mandi found herself pondering yet again why Trent had been such a serial cheater. She half wondered if she should try some midnight yoga herself to help her sleep.

Camila lay down prone on the floor (would she drop off right there? Surely not. The stone floor looked so hard to Mandi) and after half-a-minute raised her chest off the ground in a cobra pose. Somehow her hips narrowed and Mandi averted her eyes, in case Camila caught her staring.

The next morning, Camila was frosty and dismissive again, a sulky look souring her pretty face. She'd paled considerably. More milky-latte-skinned than cinnamon now. Mandi had avoided looking in the mirror altogether. She'd slept badly and imagined she had dark, half-crescent moons hanging under her normally heavily made-up eyes.

It was just before lunch when Mandi rounded a corner in the corridor to find Camila flattened against a wall, with a butch-looking, greasy-haired woman leaning in to her, talking right in her face. Her breath must have been hot and foul on Camila's skin. "So pretty, ain't you?" the woman was saying. "So pretty … why don't you come see me–"

"Hey," Mandi yelled, alarmed. "What are you doing? … Get AWAY from her." She felt her blood pressure rise, and knew immediately she needed to get Camila out of the situation, fast. The woman snapped her head round and brought her eyes to bear on Mandi's, making her shrink back a little. Where the hell were the prison wardens when you needed them?

"Leave. Her. Alone," Mandi spat.

The woman turned and walked off without saying another word, leaving Mandi and Camila stood stock-sill, trying to process what had just happened.

Mandi spoke first. "I think she liked you."

"Thanks for that," said Camila in small, weak voice before striding off herself. Mandi followed her into their dorm to see if she was okay, but Camila assured her she was and just wanted to be left alone.

The pair didn't properly speak until late afternoon. "How are you doing?" Mandi asked.

"Not too bad, considering. You?"

"Okay ... I guess."

Camila seemed to have thawed considerably. "Thank you, again," she said, "for earlier. That woman was a complete nutcase. Totally freaked me out."

Mandi shrugged. "No problem. I owed you one."

There was a pause, a slightly awkward, stilted silence, and to fill it, Mandi asked, "I saw you doing yoga last night. Did it help you sleep?"

"A bit. It relaxes me. I teach classes, you know."

Mandi raised her eyebrows. Trent had never mentioned that. "Where?"

"Media City. I go to a few ladies' homes, for one-on-one lessons too."

Another pause, while Mandi considered how boring she must have been in bed in comparison. An image of Camila swinging from some kind of sexual gymnasium entered her head. "D'you mind if I ask, what's happening between you and Trent?"

Annoyance flashed across Camila's face. She looked like she might strop off, then, on remembering she had no-one else to discuss her troubled lovelife with, relaxed her features and began to talk. "I just spoke to him actually."

"How is he?"

"Selling cigarettes to the inmates already. They're only allowed to buy three packs a week. Trent's getting thirty dirhams a pack from desperate smokers. Says it's awful in there, though."

"I can imagine." Mandi shuddered.

"I called off the engagement, the day we got out of Bur Dubai police station," Camila confided, twirling a strand of tawny hair round her finger. "He's cheated on me before. It's just hard to walk away from him for good."

Mandi nodded, in silent agreement. "So you're still together?"

Camila lowered her eyes. "Yes. He tells me he'll change … Did your mum make it here?" she asked politely, changing the subject.

Her sudden kindness took Mandi aback. "Yep. Just for a few days," she replied. "Had to go back for work though." A longing for her mother, for outside life, her apartment and friends, swept over her like floodwater. "Shall we see if the deck of cards is free?" she suggested, desperate for company, desperate to do something, anything, to block the painful emotions surging through her. Twenty-seven more days. *Maybe less if we're let out earlier.*

"Okay," agreed Camila with only a hint of reluctance. "No cheating! *Ha!*"

Arriving back in their dorm after a surprisingly fun card game and revolting supper, the pair walked in to find an angry ruckus going on. Two women were screaming at each other in different languages, their voices high-pitched and aggressive. Their faces grew closer then the taller lady did something that took Mandi totally by surprise: she spat in the other woman's face, flung her fist up and scratched the side of her cheek, drawing blood, which trickled in a red line from the cut.

"Stop," gasped Mandi and Camila in unison. Together, they pulled the women apart. No-one else reacted, apart from the injured prisoner who started wailing like a banshee. Wardens rushed in and Mandi saw a flash of silver under the striplight. Handcuffs. In a smooth, well-practised movement, the staff cuffed the two women and pushed them out the door.

Mandi heard metallic jangling and wails echoing away down the corridor, and couldn't stop trembling. At that moment, she felt like she'd found hell.

The mood remained tense in the room for the rest of the evening. The atmosphere was strained, expectant.

"You know what these women need to learn?" Camila whispered later.

"What?"

"Yoga."

"Well why don't you teach them?"

Camila looked thoughtful for a moment. "Maybe I will."

Just before lights out, Camila demonstrated a series of poses and encouraged their fellow inmates to have a go. At first the women looked confused, but then one joined in and slowly the others got down on the floor and tried some basic positions. Communication was difficult, but Camila got round it by using gentle, guiding hands to help her roomies comfortably stretch their limbs. An air of calm descended over the dorm. Camila smiled at Mandi, and mouthed, "It's working."

Mandi broke off from building her core strength in a dolphin pose (picturing Camila's stomach as she engaged abdominal muscles she didn't know she had) and gave an enthusiastic thumbs up.

"Now let's try a sun salutation," suggested Camila. "This is called Surya Namaskar and it's a great way to greet the day. To begin, stand in mountain pose …" She distributed her slight weight evenly over both feet, and executed a flawless salute to the sun as her unlikely pupils valiantly struggled to keep up. The Iranian prisoner collapsed to the floor in a fit of giggles, and Camila took that as her cue to bring her first class to an end. "Tomorrow night, same time," she called out after congratulating everyone for doing so well.

The next evening, there were more participants as several of the women from next-door were allowed to join them. At the end, Camila taught them a breathing exercise and then, in a smaller group composed of the keenest women, explained the art of visualisation.

"This helps to cleanse your chakras," trilled Camila, her voice clear and strong. "Ground yourself with a few deep breaths … " She inhaled then blew the air out slowly through her nose. "And now, with your eyes closed, imagine a bright halo of white light surrounding your head." Camila confidently ran through the colours she wanted her pupils to conjure up – a ball of deep red, pulled down the spine; orange pulled to the naval; a yellow ball to the solar plexus; green to the heart. "Lastly, fill the crown of your head with violet. With each colour, ask yourself: How does this colour make my body feel?" Camila turned her head slowly, surveying the confused faces of the six remaining students, and smiled triumphantly.

Mandi could see she was getting totally carried away, and it was likely most of the women hadn't understood a word. But even so, with sunshine accessible for just twenty minutes, twice a week – when, in turns, the inmates could visit a small concrete yard – the chakra exercise must have done some good.

***

Time inside dragged, the days more like weeks, the weeks like months. Keeping a routine helped. Breakfast, reading, lunch, nap, chess, cards, supper, yoga, lights out. Repeat. Knowing their jail sentence was so short was a huge boost to their morale, as was Mandi and Camila's burgeoning friendship.

The pair became inseparable. They propped each other up, made sure they both ate the vegetable broth and other meals thrown onto plates for them, did their washing together in the troughs that passed as a laundry, and kept each other's spirits up under difficult conditions.

"Never thought I'd say this, but you're alright," said Camila one night. "Just keep your hands off my boyfriend, okay!"

"You sure you really want to be with him?" Mandi replied. "You could do so much better, you know."

Mandi started a diary, which she would later attribute to keeping her sane, and vowed to turn her jottings into a book once she got out. The nightly yoga classes continued, with

Mandi helping to instruct wherever she could (she became quite flexible herself and lost half a stone). There were no more fights, at least not in their dorm, and the butch woman stayed away from Camila.

On the night before their early release, they talked about their plans for life on the outside. They were both returning to their home countries and had made a list of magazines to approach that might pay handsomely for their story. The pair hugged. "It's over!" grinned Mandi. "We've made it, alive. Can you believe it? Freedom's going to feel incredible. Where shall we go to celebrate?"

"Brunch at the Ritz-Carlton," said Camila, tears of joy welling up in her eyes.

"I'm so going to enjoy the toilets," squealed Mandi. "I can't wait!"

Their last yoga class was also an emotional affair. "Keep it up ladies, every night," implored Camila. "Remember, breathe in slowly through your nose and exhale the air through your mouth, silently repeating 'r-e-l-a-x'." If they'd made even the tiniest difference in these women's lives then it had all been worth it.

"I'm going to do it," said Camila after the class was over. She grinned broadly, a twinkle in her eye.

"What?" said Mandi.

"Tomorrow, when we're outta here – I'm going to dump Trent. There's no point. He'll only cheat on me again, especially if we're thousands of miles apart."

"About time too," said Mandi, returning her new best friend's wide smile and giving her arm a squeeze just above her rose tattoo, which Mandi planned to have inked onto her ankle as a permanent marker of their friendship before they both left Dubai for good.

Travel with Kids: The Bad and the Worse

"Please...help....me...."

Like many expat mums the world over, every year I take the children on a pilgrimage to the motherland, to reintroduce them to their grandparents, grassy fields and Wellington boots.

Most expat kids are frequent flyers, but I think it's the hollow-eyed, jet-lagged mums – many of whom have to travel long distances with their overactive offspring solo – who deserve recognition for ensuring that everyone arrives intact.

Now that my two are older, flying with them is so much easier, but I haven't forgotten what trial by two-year-old is like at 37,000 feet. During a recent flight, I found myself thinking about the various stages mums go through when taking their little ones back and forth to see family. Without much further ado, here's my take on the eight steps mothers desperately seeking serenity on board must navigate:

0-8 months
Provided your baby doesn't cry like a banshee due to earache or colic, you're relieved to discover that small infants are essentially hand luggage, and can be stored in a wall-mounted bassinet – meaning, in between feeds, you're left with plenty of hands-free time for other, adult-related pursuits.

Enjoy it. Indulge in a glass or two (while you can). This phase is over quicker than you can say pass the earplugs.

9 months-2 years
Now mobile, your infant is classed as a lap child, a burdensome phase that sees the two of you co-joined like Siamese twins and squashed into one seat.

Once sleep finally arrives (for your 30lb lead-weight bundle of joy, at least), you find yourself sitting statue-esqe – and needing the loo – as you attempt to inhale a meal and not flinch an inch in case the slightest movement rouses your child.

2-2½ years
Your toddler has progressed to a seat, but the games, toys and books you've spent days collecting are dispensed with in minutes. Fun is sought in mischievous ways: Meal tray up/tray down. Light on/light off. Window shutter open/shutter closed. Call the flight attendant. Call the flight attendant again.

When all the un-dinging you have to do gets too much, you traipse up and down the aisle – jolting several unsuspecting passengers awake as you go – or visit the bathroom together, where double-jointedness is always a plus when assisting your offspring.

2½-3 years
You've reached that murky zone where diversionary tactics are all that stand between you and a mile-high meltdown. Tantrums occur due to the most innocuous of reasons: not being allowed to bring the stroller up the aisle; the seat belt sign coming on. No other passenger makes eye contact – not even the smug mother of two crayon-loving girls opposite.

3-3½ years
By now, you're travelling with two small children – a whole new world of in-flight angst – which means that if you're on your own, losing your oldest at the airport or on board must be avoided (if you have more than two, good luck with that).

After collecting all the luggage at the other end, you feel like hugging the kind lady who, on seeing that you don't have a seventh arm to push the stroller, offers to help.

3½-4 years
Someone's told you stickers are great for keeping children entertained on board, so you're armed with sticker books. But while in the toilet, your kids stick them all over the TV. Bad idea: the heat from the screen can turn the adhesive into superglue.

Imagining the entire aircraft being decommissioned while engineers scrape Lightening McQueen and his friends off 35F's TV, you start peeling and don't stop until there isn't a single trace of sticker left. A happy coincidence is it uses up a good 20 minutes of flight time.

4-5 years
An iPad loaded with games is your saviour and, while still arriving disheveled and decorated with orange juice stains, you realise you had more time to relax on board, and even watched half a movie. A basic aviation knowledge – so as to answer questions like How does the wind move? – is extremely useful during this stage.

5 years+

You've made it. Long flights with small children no longer fill you with terror. While queuing at security, you see a mum with a seven-month-old infant struggling with all her baby paraphernalia, juggling her little one, taking her belt and shoes off, then, at the other side of the x-ray machine, pulling it all together again like a 100-piece jigsaw puzzle, and you feel like punching the air with joy that you've left the aforementioned stages well and truly behind.

Well done, you've arrived!

Sponsored by: My own personal experiences. Every.single. example.

Risky Business

By Lynn Maclean Willmoth

A highly coveted perk among families in Dubai – the holy grail for many – is being able to travel in business class with small children. Yes, your *whole* tribe, seated at the front of the aircraft, or up top in the case of the superjumbo – with acres of leg-room, fine dining and the chance for some mummy respite in the A380's on-board bar.

Finally, the day was upon us, where we could book seats for both myself and my small children in the business class cabin of the airplane taking us home.

Business class travel is indeed very special. The cabin itself seems to sparkle and twinkle with just enough 'specialness' to make anyone smile. But it's the space that's the *real* bonus. Not just the extra-large seats, or the super-big TV screens, there just seems to be enough space around you and your family to be able to settle in comfortably.

And settle in we did; the pillows a little softer, the blankets a little fluffier. I soon had both of my children cocooned into balls of happiness; Tom happy to explore the myriad of games and cartoons on offer, Lilly's little hands searching out all the extra buttons and switches not previously discovered on any seat before.

"What's this Mummy?" she asked as she picked up the console that tucks neatly into a pocket on the arm of her seat.

"Well, you can call the attendant by pushing a button here," I explain. 'But wait, if you press *here* your seat will give you a massage.' Peals of delight ensue from Lilly, already a disciple of the body rub, as she tries out all the different ways she could make her seat tickle and shudder. Was this *not* heaven? If I have a predictable difficult period with my daughter on flights it's right at the beginning, getting her to settle down. But, thanks to the wonders of the juddering seat, we're looking like the perfect family unit and I'm sipping champagne …

During our summer stay, the kids were quick to tell everyone about their trip in business class. "Oh!…*how* lovely" was the response as most pictured these tiny dots sipping wine and eating caviar – and I would watch as their eyebrows disappeared up into their hair lines.

"And what was the thing you liked *best* about travelling in business class?" they'd ask.

"The computer games," was Tom's stalwart response. The games are the same, incidentally, wherever you sit on the aircraft.

"The massage button!" squealed Lilly, "I had a massage all the way from Dubai to England!" Now, *this* was altogether *more* like the example of over-indulgence that many were on the lookout for. So on several occasions during our stay, Lilly was encouraged to repeat the story of the seat that gave her a massage and how she was going to have one *all the way back* to Dubai *too*.

On our trip home, as we board through doors at the very front of the aircraft, I immediately see that we are travelling in an older plane than the one in which we arrived. Characteristically stoic, Tom flops down into his ample seating, grabs the control and settles down for the long flight. Not so Lilly.

"Oh no, Mummy. This is *not* right!" She picks at the cover placed over the arm of her seat until it comes away in her hand only to reveal the arm of the chair.

"But where is the *thing?* Where is the massage button? I *can't* see it!" Her lip beginning to tremble just as the gangways either side of us fill up with slow moving – hmm, yes, now *stationary* – economy passengers queuing quietly to get to their seats. I sense the impending storm …

"Why don't we see what film we can find for you to watch, or maybe a game to play….?" My powers of deflection moving up into overdrive instantaneously. "Hey, do you want to look at my magazine…..? Have that chocolate bar I bought in the coffee shop just now … *how about my entire handbag?* Here, *take* it. Take a good look……!" But it was *all* in vain.

"I *want* a massage!" Lilly cries, literally cries. Huge tears rolling down her cheeks as her whole body begins to heave. All eyes are *on* us. "It's alright darling," I croon, pulling her tiny frame on to my lap, "it's not the end of the world. There *really* are worse things that can happen."

"But it *is!*" she cries, "it *is* the end of the world! I don't *want* to be on this plane. I want to get off this plane right now and get on one where I sit in a seat that GIVES ME A MASSAGE!"

Powerless to stop her, I resorted to putting my hand over her mouth in an attempt to muffle what she was actually saying. Thank heavens for the crew member (who has probably seen it all).

"Champagne madam?" she smiles, "or is that a *very large* white wine?"

The Driving Lesson

"Brake!"

    Lilibeth's stomach lurched, a sharp, deep kick that stole the air from her chest, making it impossible to breathe. Why wasn't the car stopping? Her foot pressed harder on the pedal, and the weight of her slight body rocketed through her right thigh, down her leg. A scream formed but lodged somewhere in her voicebox as the car sped up. They hurtled towards the tree faster … and faster.

    It all happened in seconds, yet seemed to unravel in slow motion. Her brain registered a male voice urgently shouting

Brake again, then the palm tree appeared in the middle of the windshield. Taller, scarier, blocking the light, the triangular pieces of brown bark like pineapple skin.

The vehicle mounted a curb and the sound of a loud splintering crash filled her ears as a tonne of hard metal ploughed into the tree. Thrown forwards, Lilibeth's hands flew up to protect her face. The seatbelt cut into her chest and shoulder, then she was jerked backwards into her seat, winded, vaguely aware of tinkling glass.

In the time it took for a titter of startled birds to take flight, her day – and possibly her job as a housemaid – shattered.

Next came silence, an extreme silence that pierced her ears with its stillness. She moved her foot off the pedal, and took a shallow, shaky breath. The airbags had deployed and a burnt-chemical smell filled her nostrils.

"Are you okay Lilibeth?"

She turned her head towards her employer. The blood had drained from his face into his neck, but he was fine. *Thank God*. So was she, physically. Her heart was pounding, but she could still feel her body, arms and legs despite the sensation of numbness spreading across her upper torso. She gave a tiny nod.

"You sure?" he asked, gentler this time. His eyes softened from marble to grey as he saw how shocked she was.

"Yes … I'm so sorry. I don't know what happened." A sob welled up her throat and she fought it down. *Don't cry. Don't cry. Not in front of Sir.* All he'd been doing was teaching her to drive so she could run the kids around, and somehow she'd crashed his enormous car into one of the only palm trees in the empty car park. She could have *killed him*. She started trembling harder.

"You slammed your foot on the accelerator instead of the brake," he said. His tone was serious, but he wasn't shouting at her, like her last Sir did when she accidentally washed and shrunk his favourite dry-clean-only shirt.

"I'll have to call the police," he said, swinging the car door open and climbing out.

Lilibeth watched as he strode round to the front of the vehicle and frowned. This wasn't happening, it couldn't be happening. The small, terrified voice in her head was reprimanding. *Now look what you've done. Gone and ruined everything by getting arrested.* Lilibeth swallowed. She drew in another deep breath, willing herself to stay calm. But there appeared to be a bird trapped in her ribcage, flapping wildly. The police could deport her … and then … It didn't bear thinking about. All the money she sent home would dry up, her son wouldn't be able to go to school. The clothes, books, food – it would all stop. Her whole family in the Philippines depended on her salary.

She sat still, her mouth pressed against a balled-up fist, heart thumping at the base of her throat, tears threatening to spill. A sharp, metallic taste crept up from her stomach. She was filled with a strange urge to run – but to where? If she fled, she'd definitely be deported.

Sir got his phone out and made a call, gazing at the front of the car, running his hands through his hair. The damage must be bad. She got out, closing the door carefully behind her, to see for herself. Glass crunched underfoot as she joined him beside the twisted bonnet. Mangled metal stared back at her. The headlamps were smashed, and the crunched registration plate lay on the ground, upside down. The car had fared worse than the tree.

She had no idea how much the garage would charge for repairs, and feared her salary would be docked for at least five years. Twenty years if she was deported and had to take a factory job in the Philippines. Lilibeth was silent, waiting for Sir to tell her the police were coming to arrest her.

"Might be a write-off," he muttered under his breath. His hand raked through his hair again, then he turned to her and said in a brighter tone, "Right, I've called you a taxi. I'm going to have to say it was me driving so you can't be here when the police arrive." He glanced at his watch. "It's pick-up time, anyway, so you can take the taxi straight to school and bring the girls home."

"So, I won't … I won't be arrested?" she stammered. An ocean of relief washed over her, making her feel even weaker than she already was.

"Arrested? No, of course not. It was an accident Lilibeth. A mistake. I should have intervened, but it all happened too fast." Regret flickered across his ashen face. "It's only a car. No one got hurt."

Lilibeth lowered her eyes, imagining how much worse it could have been.

"The only reason I'm calling the police is I need a police report, for the insurance." He laid a hand on her shoulder. "Lilibeth, are you sure you're alright? You might be in shock."

"Am fine, Sir," she lied. Nausea struck and she dug her hand into her pocket, looking for a tissue in case the feeling didn't pass.

"Here's some money for the taxi," he said, pulling a fifty-dirham note from his wallet and handing it to her. He gave her a reassuring smile. "Take it easy this afternoon, okay."

***

Sir was a kind man. Lilibeth thought about how lucky she was to have such a considerate employer as she perched on the middle hump of the taxi's back seat. Her precious charges were buckled in firmly on either side of her. The nausea had gone but she still felt stunned and shaky. Her neck hurt and the girls' high-pitched chatter permeated only the edge of her hearing. Not only was it the last day of term, but they'd never been picked up from school in a taxi before and thought it was the height of excitement.

Sir had always been respectful to her. He was the one who paid her salary each month (£370), and gave her money for babysitting. She was pretty sure his wife didn't know he was putting extra dirhams her way for all the evenings she spent watching their children while they dined out with friends.

Back at home, Lilibeth took two Panadols to ease the whiplash and kept busy tending to the girls' needs. It was her natural inclination to work hard and the girls were demanding, wanting snacks, drinks and attention. By the time Ma'am came home from work, she had them all ready for bed, in freshly laundered pyjamas, their golden hair combed until it gleamed, four rows of teeth brushed. They smelt soapy and clean.

"Thanks Lilibeth. You can go now," said Ma'am, dismissing her for the evening. Her tone was brittle, business-like. She didn't mention the car, and appeared to be looking straight past her.

It wasn't that she didn't like the girls' mother – it was more a case of treading carefully around her mood swings. And gritting her teeth every time Ma'am took credit for her work. That happened a lot. Lilibeth would spend ages in the kitchen preparing dinner then Ma'am would sit at the table, looking glowing and happy when everyone said how delicious it was. The reality was she rarely cooked. On Lilibeth's only day off, Friday, the family ordered take-out. She knew this because she carried the pizza boxes out to the rubbish first thing on Saturday morning as Ma'am slept in to recover from her hard week.

Lilibeth felt so dreadful that going out on her usual Thursday night trip to Satwa was the last thing she wanted to do. Instead, she quietly let herself out the side gate and went up the street to her friend's tiny room to tell her about her terrible day.

When she crept back into the house through the back door, she heard raised voices. Sir and Ma'am were arguing.

"I told you it was a bad idea to teach her to drive."

"No you didn't. You said it would be useful. C'mon, she's done so much for us. We agreed it was time to give something back to her, give her a new skill–"

"Well, I don't want her driving the children around. I don't think she's cut out for it."

"She was getting better. She was beginning to get it." Sir paused, and Lilibeth held her breath listening, imagining Ma'am inspecting her freshly polished nails with pursed lips. She tiptoed to her room as the row escalated.

"She crashed our car Pete. Doesn't that tell you it WAS A VERY BAD IDEA."

"Be nice to her, okay. She was really shaken up. The last thing she needs is you blaming her. It was partly my fault. I should have stopped it happening."

"So why didn't you?"

"I didn't want to grab the steering wheel in case we rolled over. For God's sake Christie, have a heart."

"Have you thought about how much this is going to cost us? How many lessons it'll take before she even passes the test?" Ma'am shot back. She carried on before Sir had a chance to answer. "How long until the car's fixed anyway?"

"A month. If they don't write it off–"

"And what if the insurance people – or the POLICE – find out you lied about who was behind the wheel?"

Lilibeth couldn't stand to hear anymore. Self-condemnation had begun to pinch like a cramp in her side. When Sir had offered her the chance to learn to drive, she'd jumped at the idea with enthusiasm, even though the thought of transporting the girls to their endless activities, their swimming and tennis lessons, their ballet classes, on Dubai's roads daunted her. She'd wondered if she'd even be able to see over the dashboard. But quietly determined to gain a new skill, she'd imagined herself buying a small second-hand car in the Philippines and proudly driving her own family around. To the fish market. The beach. The hospital for her diabetic mother's medical appointments.

She'd gone and blown that, hadn't she? There was no way she'd get her licence now. *Why was I so stupid?* She was about to put her pillow over her head in shame when she heard the words she'd been dreading.

"Wouldn't it be better if we hired a driver instead," said Ma'am. "The girls don't really *need* a nanny now they're getting older."

***

The family left that weekend for their annual Easter ski holiday in France and Lilibeth woke up on Sunday morning alone in their huge, empty house. She made a pact with herself to clean the villa until it sparkled so they'd see how much more useful she was than a driver. Her plan was to make herself indispensible, show them how much they still needed her.

Her moody Ma'am aside, she had a good deal with the Edmonton-Blythe family. Her situation was so much better than her last job in Hong Kong. There, she'd had to sleep in the children's room, on a flimsy mattress, so she could tend to the baby all night. She'd risen before dawn to start work and had been kept on her feet until midnight if the family were entertaining.

She'd stuck it out for a year, trying to see it as training, but in reality was terribly homesick, weeping most nights from the pain of being separated from her own six-year-old son. He was now eleven and almost taller than her.

Before tackling the cleaning, she switched on her laptop to Skype her family. Her computer, an older, clunky model given to her by Sir, took a while to boot up, and she looked at her watch, checking the time difference. It was nearly eight in the morning in Dubai, which meant it was just before noon in the Philippines. She was a few minutes early.

Her eagerness to see her son's face always had a strange effect on her, an unsettling mix of nerves and anticipation. What if he wasn't there? Or didn't want to talk to her? Did he really understand why she wasn't present in his life? What kind of mother was she to show love through money transfers, cardboard freight boxes and annual visits home? A few times recently he'd been out with friends instead of waiting at the brand new computer she'd spent three months' wages on and carried back to the Philippines for him.

She often questioned the sacrifice she'd made, but then she'd had little choice – his father had left when he was a baby, and she had to support him somehow.

At last, the inside of her childhood bamboo home filled the screen. The picture was blurred at first, and wonky, but came into focus as Lilibeth peered closer. The lady staring back looked much older than her fifty-three years, her complexion slightly sallow, greying hair tied into a neat bun at the back of her head.

"Lilibeth! *Kamusta ka na mahal*?" Her mother's face, out of sync with the sound, broke into a broad smile.

She grinned back. "Hi Mum! I'm okay, how are you?"

"Good. We just got back from church. I'm cooking *adobo* for everyone."

A pang of longing swept through Lilibeth – she missed her mum's cooking and could almost smell the aroma of browning, marinade-soaked chicken.

"How was the service?"

Her mother said it was excellent, and listed all the family members from their village who'd attended. Mostly Lilibeth's aunts and great aunts, as nearly all of the younger generation were employed overseas – particularly the women, their caring nature and affection for children put to domestic work in expat households the world over. Beyond her mother's shoulder, Lilibeth could see the silver crucifix mounted on the back wall and the sheet separating the main room from a sleeping area, but there was no sign of her son.

She asked if the recent rain would affect the rice harvest, then brought the conversation round to Crisanto's whereabouts.

"He's here," said her mother, and turned to call him. After a pause, he entered the room and sat next to his grandmother, a shy smile spreading across his face. Lilibeth reached out and touched the screen, yearning to stroke his face rather than the glass. She blew him a kiss, gazing at the soft curve of his cheek where it reflected light from the window. He waved back but said nothing. It always took him a while to warm up, and Lilibeth saw her mother nudging him to talk.

"Hey Mama."

"Hello my Crisanto. I miss you. How's your weekend going?"

"Okay," he shrugged.

"School's nearly out – you excited?"

He gave an enthusiastic nod. A strand of black hair had fallen into his eyes and with his hand he pushed it back off his forehead, which Lilibeth noticed was beaded with sweat. "Is it very hot?" she asked, knowing the answer was yes and that she was lucky to have an air-conditioned room with a box-spring bed. Her family spent airless nights sleeping on handwoven mats on the floor.

They talked about Crisanto's cousins, his friends and his plans for the school holiday, then her mother leaned forwards and asked how the driving lessons were going.

"Fine," said Lilibeth, feeling herself blush. "I haven't been on the roads yet – you should see the traffic here!" she added, trying to stay upbeat. She wasn't going to tell them about the crash, not when they were so proud of her for learning to drive, and so hopeful that one day she'd buy the family a car. "Is there anything you need?" she asked, changing the subject before the heat rising in her cheeks gave her away.

Her mother's face grew animated. "Actually, yes." She turned to Crisanto and they both laughed. "Go on, you ask her."

There was a pause.

"*Mama*, you know how *Iola* loves to sing?" Crisanto smiled at his grandmother.

"Yes. I do." It was true. Lilibeth's best memories were of her mother singing to her as a child. They never went to movies or travelled, but had often attended singing contests, and there was always music at family birthday parties and on national holidays. She'd grown up surrounded by singing. Lilibeth's heart strings tugged at the warm, hazy memories and she gazed longingly at the two eager, lit-up faces staring intently at her across the miles. The picture froze for a moment, then came back all jerky.

"Say that again," said Lilibeth, straining to hear. Crisanto had reddened, his embarrassment about asking for items costing money never far from the surface.

"I really want you to buy *Iola a* karaoke machine," said her son sheepishly.

"Well – what a great idea! Maybe next month's pay check will cover it." Lilibeth put a brave face on as they said their goodbyes and I love yous. She hung up, savouring the captured image on the screen of her mother and Crisanto, and with a heavy heart snapped her laptop shut.

***

Lilibeth began cleaning in earnest, hoping it would distract her from worrying about losing her job. She mopped until the floor shone, vacuumed, dusted, polished, cleaned the windows and mirrors, and swept the stairs. She was standing at the kitchen sink, about to disinfect the dishcloth, when she noticed the gardeners had arrived outside.

    The family had employed the same gardeners for several years. She'd grown quite attached to them during this time, and always took water and snacks out for them. They didn't have much English and weren't particularly skilled, but they were nice to the girls, and had kept the garden not just alive but pristine in extreme temperatures for three long, hot summers. They had few tools and worked with their hands, scrabbling around in the dirt with their fingers to plant flowers. Watching the gardeners toil away with beads of sweat rolling down their foreheads always made her thankful her job was indoors.

    She filled a bottle with water, grabbed some crisps and slipped her feet into her flip-flops by the door, leaving the slippers she wore round the house on the step. The younger, assistant-gardener saw her and waved. They managed a conversation in pidgin English and she was about to get back to the cleaning when she saw the head gardener cutting a bush a little too enthusiastically. They'd always had a tendency while trimming to scalp greenery until it was totally bare, until the twisted branches left behind were stark against the blue sky.

    "I don't think he should do that," she said, alarmed. There were leaves fluttering to the ground. Sunlight filtered through the foliage.

    "What?" asked the assistant landscaper.

    "Ma'am hates it when you cut too much. She'll go nuts."

    Lilibeth was remembering the time they'd shorn the trees along the back wall into lollipops, and Ma'am had been so cross. Another memory flashed into her mind – the time they bludgeoned a water pipe while toppling some Damas trees. After four hours with no water, the head garden man announced with a megawatt grin: "It's fixed!" Funnily, his head scarf had disappeared – a fact Ma'am did not find amusing at all. In fact, she'd nearly burst a gasket.

"I really think you should tell him to stop," she said as she watched the bush being pruned to within an inch of its life.

The young man in front of her shrugged. He didn't call out to his boss to stop. He told her they weren't coming back. "Finished," he said with another shrug. "Halas. Ma'am gave us notice – two weeks ago. Today is last visit."

"Why?" asked Lilibeth, feeling the small hairs on the back of her neck rise.

"No idea … no reason given."

He didn't seem particularly bothered, although he said he'd miss all the snacks she supplied, and the girls. Strange that Ma'am hadn't mentioned it, Lilibeth thought. Sir hadn't said anything either.

***

Satisfied that the house was spic and span, Lilibeth went out the next day to visit a friend in Jumeriah. They used to be neighbours, but Riza's employers moved house and she now lived far away. Lilibeth rode three buses to get there, crossed Jumeriah Beach Road when the steady flow of traffic allowed, then ducked down a side street between a cosmetic surgery centre and a cake shop.

The road was lined with white villas, each with a garden flaunting bougainvillea in technicolour and sweet-smelling frangipani. It was a relief to get away from the silence of the house, and breathing deeply, Lilibeth caught a waft of soothing jasmine. It was the calmest she'd felt since crashing the car, the weight on her shoulders, the blame and guilt momentarily relieved.

She recognised the villa where Riza worked from photos of the front garden. The family had put in a small pool and water feature, sculpted around large boulders imported from Tibet.

Riza had plenty of time to meet her as her employers were travelling, and their grown-up children had left home. The dogs she was paid to look after began barking as soon as Lilibeth slipped inside the gate. The sprinklers were on, and as she walked past the meticulously manicured lawn she felt a mist of water lightly wetting her ankles.

Riza lived in a much-coveted room, a low-roofed, detached outhouse in the garden, so she had her own door, as well as a plasma TV with all the Filipino satellite channels. Even so, there still wasn't room to swing a cat. Ushering Lilibeth inside, she beckoned for her to sit on a wicker chair, and Lilibeth flopped down gratefully, removing her flip flops, lifting her legs and hugging her knees to her chest. "I'm such an idiot," she cried, tension welling behind her eyes again. "I think I'm going to lose my job."

The sorry tale of her car crash, the overheard row and the unexpected dismissal of the gardeners came tumbling out. Tears escaped from the corners of her eyes and she used the pads of her finger and thumb to wipe them away. Rizza passed her a tissue. "If I'm sacked, " said Lilibeth, sniffing, "I won't be able to afford to buy my family the karaoke machine they've set their hearts on, let alone a car."

Riza gave her a hug. "But you could always get another job."

"I don't want another job. It was all going so well. I was going to get my licence ... Sir said my driving was getting loads better, until I made that dumb mistake. I love the girls. Ma'am can be huffy but she works long hours so she's gone most of the day–" The spectre of her last job loomed large in her mind again. Her previous employers had only given her one day off *a month* and frequently sent her out to clean the homes of rich relatives when she was meant to be resting. She was terrified of ending up in a similar situation.

Riza's voice cut into her thoughts. "I'd quite like a new job myself?"

"Really?" said Lilibeth, looking up in surprise. "Why?"

"Time for a change."

"Has something happened? Surely you'd never find a better job than this? Look at your wardrobe for a start." Lilibeth could reach the closet from where she was sitting and opened the door. It was filled with designer clothes, from Zara and Burberry, her stylishly dressed Ma'am's cast-offs.

"I'm a bit annoyed about something." She raised a dark, neatly plucked eyebrow. "I'm going home next month, and they've booked me on Cebu Pacific."

"Which is a problem … because?" said Lilibeth, confused.

"It's the low-cost carrier. I've always flown Emirates in the past – the baggage allowance is much better."

Lilibeth threw her head back and laughed. Her friend had become so spoiled after twelve years in Dubai.

By the time she left, she was feeling much more cheerful. Riza had promised her that, if she did quit, she'd recommend her for the job, and it was such a boost to hear that there were other jobs out there with generous families. Possibly even a new career as a nursery assistant.

***

With time to spare, Lilibeth headed to the beach. The dry desert heat gave way to a refreshing ocean breeze, and the vast expanse of water made her feel reflective. Further out at sea, there was a swell, like a muscle under the surface. *Change is difficult,* she thought, *but being sacked isn't the end of the world.*

Sitting down on the sand, she stared at the waves gently chafing the line of seashells. The tide was coming in, and she shuffled backwards a little, digging her toes into the cold underlayer of sand. If she listened hard enough, it was as though the gulls and the waves were singing to her.

When her phone beeped, it pulled her out of her hypnotic state with a start. She pulled her mobile from her pocket and looked at the screen. It was Sir.

"We're in the hospital. Christie broke her leg ski-ing. She's being operated on, and will be out of action for a while. I'm looking into a course of intensive driving lessons for you. I hope this is OK? Christie is going to need driving to hospital appointments and physiotherapy in Dubai. I'll make sure you're compensated for your extra duties. Regards, Pete"

Lilibeth reread the message, barely able to believe the news. Not only would she keep her job, but she'd also get proper fast-tracked driving lessons and a pay rise. She'd get her *licence*. She'd be able to buy her family a karaoke machine, and in a few years' time, maybe even a car.

A jolt of pleasure shot through her solar plexus and she was about to punch the air in triumph when a small, inner voice reminded her Ma'am was probably in pain.

She raised her eyes to the cloudless blue sky and gazed at the pale white glow of the moon, already visible high above the horizon. The same round moon shining on her family in the Philippines, a fixed point connecting them and controlling the tide now playfully kissing her sand-covered feet. She flexed her ankles and legs, wiggled her toes in the foam, then turned her eyes back to the expansive sky and whispered *Thank you!*

As excuses go, it's a good one. Watertight. I could make a U-turn now, go straight to the office. Would anyone really notice if I didn't turn up? I push my sunglasses higher on my nose, my gaze glued to the seven lanes of traffic travelling along at dramatically different speeds. And, anyway, who in the world meets before eight am? Other than CEOs and directors?

Mothers, of course.

As it happens, I fall into both camps.

I've just waved Jacob off to school on the bus and really ought to be on my way to work. Instead, I'm driving to the class coffee morning, wondering what I'm letting myself in for. Competitive catering at best, a nest of vipers at worst. It's the first meet-up of the new school year, and I'm going because I've vowed I'll be a more active parent this term (without becoming class mum – as mentioned, I have an excuse. Honestly).

Realising I'm lost and the Arabian-design, turreted villas lining the leafy street have two different numbers on them, I call Host Mum for directions. Her beautiful, enormous, zillion-dirham home is the venue for our get-together and she guides me through the rabbit warren that is the Green Community. "So nice of you to grace us with your presence," she trills down the phone, straight into my inner ear, and it hits me that I'm now committed.

Once inside, she leads me to a table laden with pastries, croissants and macarons in every colour – prepared, I suspect, at the same time as jiggling her toddler, child number three, on her hip and flawlessly applying mascara. She smells like the perfume department of Harvey Nichols, a heady mix that wafts around her like a cloud.

"Help yourself," she says, handing me a plate with a fancy napkin on top. From the sofa, a peel of laughter rises from the women already seated, a tinkling noise that floats over like a stream of bubbles.

The interior of her villa is astonishing. All clean lines, gleaming floor tiles and rich Persian carpets, illuminated by floor-to-ceiling windows, through which the blue of a sparkling pool is visible. Every surface that could be French-polished or topped with marble has been so, and the light-filled room we're comfortably gathered in is crowned by an elegant, eye-watering chandelier. It's hard not to gawp with envy. I catch sight of a gardener outside, then the family's housemaid watering the plants, and my social conscience kicks in like a slap on the face.

As I reach for a tartlet crowned with jewel-like fruit, Host Mum whips off a silver, dome-shaped food cover to reveal a perfect Victoria Sponge cake.

The meet-the-mums coffee morning is never as easy as just nattering with all the mum friends you already know, because the classes are mixed up each year. Plus September sees numerous new arrivals to Dubai.

Scanning the room, I spot someone I recognise. Swiss Mum, who always looks effortlessly chic in designer clothes. She raises her hand and waggles her fingers, her bobbed hair softly framing her sun-kissed face.

I wave hello back, but it's too late to make chit-chat. Host Mum is inviting us to sit in a circle and tell each other a little bit about ourselves, including what we used to be.

Among our group – from places as diverse as Germany, Australia, Jordan and South Africa – there's a lawyer, a banker, a child-protection officer and a social worker. But none of them working, because everyone has given up their careers to become a "trailing spouse" (ie, husband gets well-paid job overseas, wife and family pack their bags to follow).

To fill their time, they're setting up uber-stylish homes in Dubai, caring for children full-time and protecting their young like tigresses. I almost apologise when it's my turn to speak. I clear my throat and announce to the group that, ah-em, I'm an editorial director, for a business magazine. Full-time.

There's a moment of silence, and then someone says, "Goodness, how do you juggle everything?"

"With a lot of help," I say, and let out a nervous laugh.

The conversation moves on to the finer details of our children's lives at the international school Jacob attends. All very interesting, especially as my son always tells me he does "nothing", and rather humbling, because I haven't actually been into school yet this term. Never mind where the kids get changed for swimming, I'm not exactly sure where the new classroom is, and the teacher is still emailing my husband rather than me.

But this is all going to change. I just have to get through the next few weeks at work. Then it should calm down. I glance at my watch. Eight fifty. I really need to get going soon.

I nod in agreement when the mums promise to not try to outdo each other when it comes to our children's birthday parties (Phew, Jacob's is first, the stakes won't be too high. No life-size piñatas, mini-funfairs or pony rides for us!). And I attempt to enter a debate about what kind of cupcakes to send in for the bake sales.

Note to self: Open my cupcakes-that-have-never-been-made folder this year.

Then, as we discuss having a BBQ to get the dads together, the Christmas party, fundraisers and playdates for younger siblings, I find myself thinking, "I really don't know how these women do it!" Life is so much easier in the office.

At least it would be if the sales team were actually selling ads, and our conferences weren't being cancelled due to a precipitous drop in interest. But, as I said, it's just a blip. Things will get better; I'll have more time soon for Jacob, for making cakes.

"So," says Host Mum, "the last thing on the agenda – any volunteers for class mum?"

I lower my eyes, and only look up when a lady dressed in brightly coloured clothes offers to take on the role. Mercury red hair tumbles over her shoulders. I know her as Drama Mum; last year she gave up her time to run acting classes for the children and directed a production of Annie. She cheerfully tells us she's already the coordinator for two other classes. "All three of my daughters want me to be class mum," she says with a chuckle, "so it's no problem."

A case of Stockholm Syndrome? I wonder.

Collective sighs of relief resonate around the room and Host Mum rises to her feet to start collecting up the china mugs and teapot, sitting on a shiny, silver, engraved tray that looks suspiciously like bling.

***

As I arrive at the office, my PA is standing by my desk, writing on a yellow Post-it note, which she sticks on my monitor. "Oh hello," she says, on seeing me. She flicks her hair over her shoulder. Debbie moved to Dubai because she couldn't stand the weather in London. Every inch of her is firm from working out with a personal trainer, and a deep suntan adds a finishing touch to it all. "CNN just called," she says. "They asked if someone could be available for an interview tonight. I said you'd ring back."

"Thanks Debbie." I glance at the number she's written on the Post-it, and know immediately it'll mean I might not make it home in time for Jacob's bedtime. Something cold clutches my heart, and I try to ignore the feeling as I call the producer and agree to come to the TV studio for six thirty.

The morning disappears in an avalanche of work, and before I know it my stomach is growling for food. I put the feature I'm editing to one side and massage my forehead.

"Julie."

Startled, I open my eyes. "Yes. What is it?" Debbie is standing in front of me.

"Erm, HR mentioned you're eligible for a grooming appointment before your TV interview this evening." Debbie smiles. "So I've booked you in at Tips & Toes at three. Eyebrow threading and nails."

What? My head pops up. I know I'm not the most polished person, but I don't exactly get much time to go to the salon.

"Is that ... okay?" says Debbie, giving me an appraising look. She bats her thickly mascaraed eyelashes. "Just think of it as 'me time'," she says with another smile.

"That's fine," I nod, wincing. Bang go my plans to finish my monthly board report this afternoon. I'll have to burn the midnight oil to get it done tonight. Just like I did last night, and the night before. As Debbie turns on her Jimmy Choo heel and walks away, I take a large bite of my sandwich and chew it without really tasting it.

***

The super-comfy chairs at Tips & Toes are so padded and inviting I sink into a seat gratefully and slip my feet out of my shoes. Rose, my beauty therapist, peers closely at my eyebrows and frowns.

"When did you last have them threaded?"

I think for a moment. "Um … a while ago. I've been busy. Work … my son, too much to do," I say defensively. Rose looks concerned, as though I've personally affronted her and she might even cry. "I won't leave it so long next time," I promise.

Rose dabs at my overgrown eyebrows with a babywipe. "Too much," she tuts. "Too much! Oh. You have hair here too. You want removed?" she says, rubbing my upper lip with her finger. "I can wax your moustache."

"No, thank you," I reply, wondering what on earth happened to good old-fashioned flattery in Dubai's beauty salons.

"Maybe next time," she says helpfully.

I use both hands to pull the skin around my eyebrow taut and she inflicts the cotton-twisting treatment on me. I flinch, and my left eye starts streaming. Before she can do the other brow, she waits patiently while I sneeze randomly and wipe away the tears forming in the corner of my eye. I don't relax until both brows are done and she's applying soothing aloe vera gel. The last thing I want is to look like my forehead has broken out in hives under the bright light of the TV cameras.

"Ma'am, we have a new cream you might like," says Rose in her soft voice. "A wrinkle cream."

I decline, and it's a relief when Rose moves on to administer pain to someone else. Another slight, dark-haired therapist starts working on my nails.

"I did mention that I don't have much time," I say politely. "Could you just do a quick buff and polish please?"

She inspects my nails and twists her face into a grimace. It's that frown again. I wonder if they're taught the frown at beauty school. Now she's solemnly shaking her head. "Ma'am, your nails are cracked. I fix for you?"

Ok, so I bite my nails. Just two of them. It's a nervous habit I'm not proud of. But when the pressure at work gets too much, and no one's watching, my forefingers drift to my mouth. Usually the left hand as my other hand is generally occupied, holding my phone or a pen.

I realise my technician is waiting for an answer, and nod. "Okay, but I really do need to be done by four, please." I give her my best I'm-not-at-all-stressed smile and she gets started as though she has all the time in the world.

When my phone rings it sounds loud and shrill in the empty salon.

"I'd better get that," I say. "Sorry!" The nail lady carries on with the other hand while I listen to Debbie's fluty voice telling me what not to wear at the TV studio.

I glance at the clock on the wall. Three forty-five.

I don't know how anyone has time for a full one-hour manicure. All that filing and shaping and cuticle-pushing while sitting in one spot, unable to do anything with your hands. Unable to respond to messages, write notes, edit or type.

Feeling on edge, I practise answers in my head. The producer has already told me what they're going to ask – will the low oil price affect real estate? But there's always the chance they'll go off-script, and as the spokesperson for the Middle East's version of The Economist, it doesn't look good on camera if you're caught like a deer in the headlights.

I look up and see my technician staring at me again, expectantly. "Which colour, Ma'am?" Her eyebrows are raised. I must have not heard her the first time. What colour did Debbie say I should wear? A solid colour. Definitely not white. And not red, which can bleed on screen. Does it really matter? The economy's heading for recession and the energy giants are shedding jobs. Whole layers of middle-management are being stripped out, and regional banks are cutting staff, too. It seems incongruous sitting here choosing nail polish. "Perhaps a neutral tone?" I suggest, eyeing the little pots lined up behind her.

She gets up and brings a selection of nail varnishes over, setting them down on the tray with a clink. "This one," I say with a smile, aware that my phone's just bleeped and my fingers have turned into rigid sticks.

A streak of irritation flashes through me like electricity as I scan the message – I know the deadline for the figures is today. I was up all hours working on the damn report. They'll have it, by five.

Rose reappears, carrying a tray of folded, soft, white towels. She stops next to me and smiles. "Did you know about our special offer this month?"

"What's that?" I ask, trying to rearrange my face into an interested expression.

"Thirty-five per cent off a massage if you spend more than 150dhs. Would you like me to make you an appointment?"

"Erm, that's okay. I'll need to check my diary."

"Are you sure? We could fit you in this afternoon." She gives me a thoughtful look. 'You look a little … stressed."

Why is the nail lady nodding? I've been sitting still, getting nothing done, for forty-five minutes now. Isn't that enough to make anyone stressed?

"I'll book an appointment soon," I say. "After work calms down. It's all a bit crazy right now." Just a blip. *Could we just get my nails finished so I can get out of here?*

Satisfied with my answer, Rose starts transferring the towels into an alcove and I watch the colour going onto my nails in smooth, shimmery, ballet-slipper-pink strokes.

The sound of my phone not only noisily ringing again but also vibrating on the side table fills the salon. Rose's head spins round at the same time as the nail lady's hand stops in mid-air, holding the brush. They're both regarding me with quizzical expressions, watching like hawks to see what I do next. I lift my shoulders into a tiny shrug, and without moving my gleaming-wet nails a millimetre, obediently say, "It's okay, they can leave a message."

Rose makes a clicking noise with her mouth, and my fingers itch – literally itch – to answer my phone.

From inside my bag comes another ringtone. An impossibly jaunty tune, erupting on my other mobile. The one I use for family, friends and close contacts. Damn. What if it's school? Or my driver? I can't think now for ringtones. I'm all twitchy and alert.

"Could you, perhaps … answer that?" I say pleadingly to Rose. My palms flat on the cushion, I crane my neck and nod at my bag. "It's just in the side pocket … Thank you!"

The throbbing sensation shooting down my arms recedes as she shows me the caller display (the sales director) and tells him I'll ring back in ten minutes. As soon as my nails are dry.

I can see the other therapists looking over pityingly. Their eyes darting glances at me, the woman who can't stop working, who can't relax even for a manicure.

***

When I took this job, it freaked me out that it involved such long hours and travel around the region. I deliberated over whether to accept the promotion, and decided I'd give it a go. If it all got too much, I'd step back. The decision was probably made for me during my maternity leave, when I found myself not only dealing with a screaming, colicky baby, but also feeling restless and unproductive.

I spent the first two weeks loving every moment of getting to know Jacob. Then, when the learning phase and visitors subsided, and the evening bouts of crying became worse, I started wondering what to do with the pockets of free time that naps provided.

I began using the Excel spreadsheets I routinely applied to work problems to chart Jacob's first few months. He was only really content when I held him upright. When I presented my Excel diary to a gastroenterologist, he initially thought I was nuts. After reading it, he agreed with me that the issue was more than just colic. Jacob had acid reflux and once it was treated, the screaming stopped. My agitation with staying at home didn't get any better, however.

At first, combining the job and motherhood worked out great. I'd have these really busy days and come home and a whole different thing would start. During my evenings with Jacob, my pace and goals changed. Nothing was predictable. The whole world worked differently. It all centred around Jacob.

Now that he's nearly seven, things aren't working out quite so well. In the last fortnight alone I've felt guilty more times than I can remember. I had to pack Jacob off to school with a bad cold because I needed to travel for work; I've got ongoing guilt about failing an old friend whose mother recently died; and then there's the guilt about all the out-of-hours gigs I end up doing – the evening drinks, weekend conferences – when I should be doing something fun with my son.

The truth is, I'm frazzled and stretched too thin.

***

Arriving at the TV studio, I'm ushered straight to hair and make-up. A young girl with dark hair tied in a long ponytail approaches me and introduces herself as Natalie. "We haven't got much time," she says, peering at my face for slightly longer than feels comfortable, "so I'm just going to apply some foundation to make you look less washed out."

"Okay," I say. I steal a glance at myself in the mirror. She's right. I am pale. Some might even say a bit gaunt.

"You know, it's not a good idea to avoid the sun entirely," she advises. "Lots of women in the UAE, especially local ladies who cover, are deficient in vitamin D because their skin never sees the sun."

She continues chatting as she brushes my hair so it looks tidy and then liberally squirts hairspray at the front and back while I shield my eyes. "Now let's give you some colour," she says, smoothing a beige cream over my cheeks, chin and forehead. It's brighter than anything I'd ever use myself, and gives me a bronze, radioactive glow. She pays special attention to my under-eye area. "There," she says, looking pleased with herself. "Eyebags gone."

A woman with a clipboard arrives and takes me to the green room, unapologetically telling me on the way that my segment is delayed as the other interviewee is stuck in traffic. "Just relax for a while," she suggests, all straight, white teeth, and glossy, plumped-up lips. "I'll get you some magazines."

Relax? Is she serious? I'm about to go on live TV, and now there's no way I'll get home in time to put Jacob to bed. Reluctantly, I pull out my phone and text John. He replies with three words, *OK good luck*, and guilt washes over me again that I'm not there. A minute later, another text arrives. *We'll be watching*.

When clipboard lady returns, she whisks me down the corridor to the studio. We wait outside until the red 'on air' light goes off then she pushes the double swing doors open and I follow her in. The studio lights are dazzling and I blink several times as my eyes adjust. "Mind the cables," she says, and leads me over to a panel where I'm invited to sit. A female floor manager threads a microphone wire under my blouse and clips it to my collar.

Sitting behind a desk on the other side of the studio is one of our biggest, and most difficult, clients, the CEO of Emirates Energy. We nod politely. The presenter says hi while simultaneously reading scripts and talking to someone via an earpiece, then looks up and launches into a quick briefing. In the corner of my eye, I see a camera swinging round overhead.

"Twenty seconds," says clipboard lady, checking her watch.

The strange thing is I don't feel the usual flurry of nerves that always creep up on me just before a live interview. I feel oddly calm. No butterflies at all. My stomach isn't flipping. Whereas before I was always excited to be on TV, this time I'm feeling really over it. I just want to go home.

"Ten seconds."

An image of Jacob comes into my mind – the sweetest, most loving boy in the world, sitting in front of the television in his Star Wars pyjamas – and for a moment I'm terrified a tear might leak from my eye and run down my powdered cheek like hot wax dripping onto a birthday cake.

"Welcome back," the presenter says suddenly, staring at the autocue. "So, has the bubble burst for the Dubai property market? Or has the emirate learnt from the debt crisis of 2007?"

He introduces us, mentions the huge housing projects that were scrapped after the last global credit crunch, and then opens up the floor for debate. All of a sudden everyone's looking at me, and I begin to speak as though I'm on autocue myself. I could talk about this in my sleep. Even so, with the camera trained on my face, I'm surprised by the lack of adrenaline. Perhaps I should have eaten something beforehand. My voice sounds strange, detached.

I squint at the lights as the CEO speaks. A slight headache has spread across my forehead. I'm so tired. So very tired. The glare is intense. Now I've lost the gist of what he's saying. Come on Julie. *Focus.*

I find my inner media mogul just as the CEO says there have been no job cuts at his firm.

What? What the hell is he talking about? I know for a fact that there have been redundancies among his staff. At least two hundred. They got paid handsomely to go quietly, keeping it all hush-hush. I almost have to pinch myself. At last, the adrenalin kicks in, and I interrupt.

"Excuse me," I hear myself saying. "You're lying! Why can't you just tell the truth for once?"

The studio vanishes for a moment, replaced by white light and a stunned silence, and then it rushes back in. Countless pairs of eyes bore into mine. Anger flashes across the executive's features and the presenter shifts awkwardly in his seat.

My armpits prickle with sweat.

Did I really just say that? Did I really just call him a liar on live TV?

My God, I did. The blood drains from my face and I feel light-headed. I swallow hard but the lump in my throat sticks like a pebble.

Despite knowing damn well I'm right, I wish I could take the words back. But they're out there now, like starlings freed from a cage. They've already been broadcast into hundreds of thousands of homes, beamed to a satellite and transmitted across the region.

As the CEO – our biggest advertiser – responds, I want to abscond to a place where I haven't just humiliated him in public, but the cameras are still rolling, the circle of lights still dazzling my eyes, the microphones picking up every sound. The interview limps on, my face so flushed with heat I'm convinced I must be beetroot red.

***

The next day, I awake feeling sick to the stomach. For a moment, I kid myself that the interview was just a bad dream. Then I sit up in bed and relive it, holding my head in my hands. A groan escapes my mouth. Why didn't I just keep my trap shut?

John is already up and walks into the bedroom with a cup of tea. He hands it to me with a tight-lipped smile. The smile quickly fades, but there's kindness in his eyes. He feels sorry for me. He knows I've made a mistake, and is trying to make it better. I sip the hot tea, scalding my tongue.

"I seriously have no idea what got into me," I say.

John sits down on the edge of the bed and takes my hand in his. "Well, you've been having problems with Emirates Energy for a while. It must have welled up from inside – and anyway, what you said was true." He shrugs. "They had it coming, if you ask me."

"Am I an overnight Twitter sensation?"

I watch his face as he gives me another half smile, his eyes clouding over. He doesn't have to say anything. I already know the answer. He passes me my phone and I quickly scan the long list of Twitter notifications.

My heart gives a thump like a punch in the chest.

"I don't want to see," I say, and hand the phone back. John walks over to the curtains and pulls them open with a scraping noise, letting light pour into the room. "I guess I'd better get up and face the music," I say quietly, aware of a knot of pain radiating through my neck and shoulders.

Slumping into my chair at work, I'm still considering the likelihood of being sued when Debbie comes over looking all grave and serious. Her skin has blanched under her suntan. "Malcolm wants to see you," she says, and I suddenly sense that she's sending me to my execution.

Like a ball of yarn unravelling in a whoosh, it happens. I lose my job. My verbal and written apologies to the CEO aren't enough.

"I'm sorry Julie," the vice-president informs me in a solemn tone. We're sitting in the boardroom, facing each other across an oval, mahogany table. "I don't want to have to do this but the impact on ad sales is going to be a massive. The magazine relies on advertising from Emirates Energy, especially with so many other firms tightening their purse strings, and CEOs don't take well to being called liars on TV," he says, shaking his head. 'I'm giving you this opportunity to resign and suggest you take the rest of the day off to think about it."

My breath catches in my lungs with a sharp jab. Five years in the job – gone overnight. My temples throb with rage. After everything I've done for the magazine. All those long hours, all the sacrifices I've made. The VP's face is closed. Hard. His mind made up. I exhale a long breath and gather up my notebook and pen, leaving the room with as much dignity as I can muster.

I go straight to the bathroom and lay my palms on the cool quartz countertop at the sink to steady myself, swallowing thickly. My mouth is dry, my head spinning. When I straighten up, I splash water on my face and compose myself.

Ding, ding, ding, ding!

More notifications arrive on my phone. All from Twitter. Apart from the last one which is a WhatsApp message from the class chat group. *Headlice confirmed in Year Two.*

***

John comes home early, with a bunch of flowers. He hugs me and tells me it's all going to be alright. "I tried calling you, but couldn't get through," he says.

"Switched both phones off," I reply with a sniff. It was either that or throw my mobiles out the window. They were continually pinging with messages about my untimely departure, headlice treatments and a lengthy conversation started by Host Mum about tennis lessons.

I hear Jacob's bus pulling up outside and the sound of the front door being flung open and then banged shut. My son does a double-take when he sees me.

"Mummy, what are you doing here?"

"Don't worry sweetheart. Nothing's wrong. I've finished work early, that's all."

After his initial alarm subsides, joy fills him like sunshine. "Can we make cupcakes?"

"Sure," I say, ruffling his hair.

It's the last thing I feel like doing – I feel like I've been in a car crash. But in need of a distraction, I pop out to the store to buy cupcake mix, butter and eggs. I walk in the late-afternoon warmth, noticing the goings on in the compound, the gardeners clipping trees, the housemaids walking dogs, kids on bikes calling to each other. A neighbour I haven't seen in months waves and I lift my hand to return the greeting. The sky is a translucent blue, the sun a golden ball, dappling the pavement with playful sunbursts.

My step feels unfamiliar, lighter than usual. What's going on? I realise it's because I'm not rushing. I can take as much time as I like at the store. I'm not on a deadline, I don't have to reply to emails or run a meeting. It's the weirdest feeling.

But I could get used to it.

Maybe – although a reproachful voice in my ear tell me it will get boring pretty quickly.

Back at home, Jacob stands on a chair at the counter, helping to stir, the pale-pink tip of his tongue peeking through his lips as he concentrates. We both poke spoons in the mixing bowl and steal licks. The uncooked buttery dough is delicious. I close my eyes to savour the taste, and when I open them, I see John standing in the doorway with a faraway look on his face.

By bedtime, I've yo-yoed up and down so many times, I'm totally wrung out. But a quiet determination has filled me. "I can do this," I say to John. "I can crack being a stay-at-home, can't I?"

He winks at me. "Of course you can."

"I'll start as I mean to go on – tomorrow Jacob won't take the bus. I'm doing the school run."

***

A line up of big cars jostle for position in the school car park. Armadas, Ford Explorers and Range Rovers all vie for space. I pull up beside a black Porsche Cayenne and step out onto sand that's been compacted until its solid by the crushing weight of tyres and feet. Jacob jumps down and we walk to the gates.

It's handbags at dawn; a catwalk of well-dressed women clutching bags and children. While my face looks pale and indistinct without make-up – and possibly a little puffy from a few tears shed first thing this morning – all the fashionista mums have apparently managed to do a full make-over. They're wearing pretty sundresses with glittery sandals, maxi dresses and jewelled flip-flops.

A new girl feeling sweeps over me like a cloak, transporting me back to my first day at secondary school as an awkward, pimply, overly studious teenager.

Catching sight of a pert bottom strutting into school in tight spandex, I realise the ones who aren't wearing dresses have donned gym wear. Black appears to be trending, with pink piping and a ponytail that swings. The over-stretched tracksuit bottoms I put on in a hurry look shabby and old in comparison.

I hear someone calling my name and turn round to see Drama Mum, her three girls trailing behind her, the smallest hidden behind a guitar. "Hey," she says brightly. "You dropping off before work today? Jacob's normally on the bus, isn't he?"

"Yes, actually …" I start, then think better of it. She doesn't need to know yet. I clear my throat. "How are you?"

"Good. Mia's off to KidZania today," she says, beaming at her middle daughter. "Oh, one moment." She calls over to another mum, giving her an important message about ballet while my attention is diverted by a seven-seater parked a hair's breadth from the gates, its hazard lights flashing, two small beacons of orange blinking nonchalantly like cat's eyes. I didn't even think you were allowed to park there. A lone, perfectly healthy-looking child climbs out with a nanny – clearly their legs would fall off if they had to walk any further.

I catch fragments of conversation going on around me, small talk. How charming the children are, how much the children are growing, how lovely everyone looks, the weather. The kids greet each member of staff manning the gate and wish them good morning. Does Jacob do that? I still feel like I'm swimming in deep water and want to put my foot on something solid that isn't there.

I kiss Jacob goodbye and tell him I'll pick him up, noticing as he scampers off that a trace of breakfast cereal, or possibly toothpaste, has made itself glaringly apparent on his bottle-green shorts.

"You sure you're okay?" asks Drama Mum, narrowing her eyes. "You look a bit off-colour."

"I'm fine," I say, my delivery a little higher than I meant it to be. "I haven't done the school run in a while … do all these women go straight to the gym?"

Drama Mum laughs. "I bet half of them don't." She lowers her voice and says conspiratorially, "Some do the pick-up in the same gym wear, creating the aura of a six-hour work out."

The fish-out-of-water feeling recedes as I decide I like Drama Mum. We could even become friends.

"I need to ask you something," she says, blowing a loose strand of raven hair out of her eyes with the corner of her mouth. "The parents' group needs some help with a newsletter. If it's not too much of an imposition … do you think I could put your name forward?"

"Sure."

"That's great, thanks! We're looking for volunteers for the winter festival too, but I'm not going to press you on that one – you must be incredibly busy with work."

"Well, yes."

I cough.

We part ways, and I walk back to the car, watching the last few mums in oversized sunglasses gliding into school with their offspring. Serenely does it. They must practise gliding.

Tomorrow, I'll get up earlier to wash my hair, and wear something smart. Possibly even heels. I own many pairs, the kind that sink in sand. They're part of my work wardrobe, my plain skirts and well-cut jackets that I now realise are totally redundant, boring and staid compared with the outfits on display at school.

Silence follows me into the house. I don't know what to do with myself for the rest of the morning. I go into the kitchen. Silent. The living room. Not a sound. It's all so quiet compared to the office. I miss the buzz of work, the chats round the water cooler. I put the radio on and take a bath.

By eleven, time has become fluid and I imagine it eddying around the furniture, dragging me slowly through the day. This is ridiculous, I've been longing for some free time for years, and now I'm at a complete loss. I have a cleaner twice a week, so there's no point doing housework, and bigger chores, like organising sock drawers and culling toys, feel beyond my energy levels.

I change clothes before heading out for the pick-up, and put some make-up on. It's hardly a glamorous look, but it'll do. I find Jacob's classroom and he cannonballs out. He's bouncing up and down with excitement, holding a brown teddy bear with a sparkly yellow bow. "It's his turn to take Bernie home," the teacher tells me. "Here, this is his scrapbook," she says, thrusting a large memory book with instructions on the front into my hands. "Have fun!"

I must have looked perplexed as she invites me to take a look at last year's book. Jacob and I read it together. The pages are filled with photos, hand-written stories, speech bubbles, decorative stamps, evidence of baking extravaganzas and even a bear-class boarding pass. My eyes widen at how creative all the entries are.

"Oh look, there's Bernie parachuting into someone's garden," I exclaim, astounded by a photo of the bear floating into the family's backyard beneath a make-shift canopy. "And here he is ON SKIS, in France!"

Bernie even spent Christmas in Lapland. There are snaps of him playing in the snow, snuggled up in a log cabin and listening to music through headsets in his airplane seat. I can almost hear the parents telling their bemused children, "*Let's take Bernie on a husky safari. Then tonight, if we're really lucky, we might get a shot of him gazing at the Aurora Borealis rolling across the sky.*"

Bernie's time with us will have a much more homely feel, I tell Jacob.

Over the next week, on top of all the usual chores and my wobbly adjustment to life post-work, I attempt to find amusing things to do with a bear. I set up numerous photo opportunities – of Bernie reading books, cosy in his pyjamas and sitting on the kitchen table eating noodles. I even remember to bring Bernie to football.

Jacob looks at me suspiciously as I secure the bear's seat belt. It's a look that suggests he thinks I've lost my mind. "Mummy, he's just a toy," he says, rolling his eyes.

I pause.

God, what has my life come to? How have I gone from editing a magazine, managing staff and budgets, and appearing on the news to mollycoddling the class bear?

Even my son is under the impression that I've lost the plot. Another few months of this and I'll have tumbleweed growing in my empty skull.

***

A note appears on the school communicator to remind parents that the following week brings Book character day – the day school is invaded by a mini fictional force of Harry Potter, Dr Seuss, Angelina Ballerina and other favourite storybook characters. My thoughts turn to costumes. This has always been John's realm. An architect by day, and creative genius in his spare time, he's been our go-to person for dress-up days from the beginning of school.

Last year, for an Easter Bonnet parade, he constructed a spring hat with a giant carrot protruding jauntily from the top, which won a prize. I tell him that this year I'll come up with something. "Won't be as good," I say, "but I'll take care of it."

"Well, let me know if you need any help," he says, grinning.

I sit at my laptop and take Drama Mum's advice to try Pinterest. I type in 'fireman costumes' and hundreds of pins come up. I scroll through these for a few minutes, then my attention begins to meander. I wonder what they're doing at work? I click on the website, where news is updated daily, and see the headlines but can't open the articles. It wants me to login. I tap in my details and freeze at the sight of the box that flashes up. *The email or password you have entered is incorrect.*

They've disabled my access. How could they? Fury flares in my chest, and I simmer with anger at the finality, the brutality of it all. I still have to go in to collect my things from my desk, and am filled with a desire to set fire to the place.

I picture the elevator, with its Elevision TV screen in the top corner; the news ticker headlines eagerly read if only to avoid eye contact with fellow blank-faced riders. I imagine the cool lobby, where the AC hits you like a breeze, and the open-plan office space, overlooking Dubai Media City, the aquamarine waters of the Gulf, the hotels and apartment blocks rising like polished teeth along the Palm Jumeriah and, in the distance, the towering Burj Khalifa. On a clear day, with no sand in the sky, you can see past Dubai's skyscrapers to the neighbouring emirate of Sharjah.

I pour myself a glass of wine in the kitchen and drain it before going back to the laptop to carry on researching costumes. So this is it. This is what my life looks like now. The three of us. Jacob chewing on his bottom lip, playing on his iPad, over the moon to have me home. John sitting in his favourite chair reading a novel. A feeling of gratefulness sweeps my outrage aside and I switch the screen back to Pinterest. I've been given this opportunity to put my family first, I remind myself, and at that moment I love John and Jacob so much I feel a tear prick in my eye.

I wait for my vision to clear and start scrolling again. The pins look just as intimidating, but surely I can rustle something up.

The trouble is I can't sew; if you handed me a piece of fabric I'd have no idea what to do with it; and the prop that would accessorise an outfit perfectly is never just lying around the house. It's usually buried at the bottom of a cupboard, lost, broken or still in the shop.

"Maybe you could wear your Spiderman top for Book Character Day," I suggest to Jacob.

"That's a film, mummy."

"Oh, yes … Perhaps last year's Halloween costume would still fit. I could colour in the skeleton to make it look like a normal pirate's outfit."

"I want to go as a dog," Jacob says finally, clapping his hand together in glee. "Floppy the dog from my phonics book. Can you make a dog costume? Please, mummy, please make me a dog suit?"

"Sure you don't need help?" chips in John.

"Nope," I say, determined, imagining the look on Jacob's face if his outfit is a laughing stock. The pressure is enough to make any otherwise sane mother start cutting up the curtains.

***

Week three of mummydom brings with it a new resolve. I attend a Parents' Group meeting and come away with ideas for a new-look newsletter. I confide to Drama Mum what's happened and volunteer to help with the Winter Festival. Out of the blue, an old contact phones with some freelance work. I'm starting to get busy, nicely busy. The quiet doesn't bother me any more. In fact, I kind of like it. I can concentrate better, and my mind no longer feels like a browser with 2,671 tabs open.

Even Book Character Day wasn't too bad in the end. Jacob went to school wearing a pair of yellow trousers, a T-shirt emblazoned with a train and a ship captain's hat – the dishevelled sum of which was intended to portray a steam train driver from his Flying Scotsman book. He seemed happy with it.

At the gate, we saw a stressed-out mother, with a teary, uniform-clad child, being asked by a teacher if they had anything at home resembling the mishmash my son was wearing. As she headed off, upset boy in tow, I gave her a sympathetic smile, and couldn't resist adding clandestinely, "Dress-up days should be outlawed, don't you think?"

For my own part, I've hit on the idea of dressing casually for the school run most of the time, then, once a term, pitching up in a ball gown. "Can you imagine the double-takes?" I laughed to John. "Priceless."

***

Deciding to do something about my waxy-white look, I take Swiss Mum's advice and book a St Tropez spray tan. A few days later, I find myself standing semi-naked in a polythene, pop-up tent, striking various poses while being squirted with a liquid the colour of black coffee.

"Eyes closed," orders a lady holding a fully loaded spray gun. She blitzes my face with a mist of fake tan. 'Turn … and turn again. Arms up … Elbows out … Face the other way."

Is this how they spray-paint cars? I wonder.

"Now lunge …"

She's so disappointed with my lunge that she does a quick demonstration, and I try again – only to step back off the towel onto the slippy bit and nearly go flying. This isn't the lying down experience I'd envisioned. The climate-controlled air and liquid tan are surprisingly cool and my skin prickles with goosebumps.

Feeling as though I'm being basted like a turkey, I let her do a second coat and, afterwards, emerge from the tent a mahogany shade.

John is waiting outside in the car. He throws his head back laughing when he sees I've taken on the appearance of a cigar.

"You look like a really well done chicken," he chortles, glancing from me to the passenger seat, clearly worried about what colour it's about to turn. I lay a towel down and climb in beside him.

"What's that smell?" he asks, noticing the distinctive biscuity scent of the fake tan. His nose crinkles.

When Jacob gets home, he tells us he preferred me when I looked like a peach. But after eight hours, and a good shower, it's toned down nicely. I glow, without an orange patch in sight. I'm rather pleased. Not least because I'll even give the school mums a run for their money.

John comes up behind me and wraps his arms around my waist. "You look lovely Julie," he says. "You really do. But I need you to come downstairs and look at something on the computer."

***

A banner headline blazes the words: 'Emirates Energy CEO fired amid corruption scandal'.

I sit down at the computer to read the article and it takes my breath away. The allegations run deep – far, far deeper than my own accusation – and have been taken seriously by the regulatory authority. The CEO has been fined and ousted for market rules violations committed during the period 2010-13. He's already been replaced by a successor, with further investigations pending.

"Bloody hell." I fold my arms across my chest. "Conducting fraudulent practices," I read aloud, "that created a misleading impression regarding the value of the company in the initial public offering stage"

I knew there was something seriously dodgy about him.

The words hang there, filling the study with their power long after the screen saver has flashed on.

"What do you think will happen now?" asks John.

"I don't know – why?"

"You might get your job back."

I exhale a long breath. A raw shiver creeps up my spine, and I'm not sure if it's anticipation or dread.

"Do you know the new CEO?" asks John.

"Yes, I've met him a few times. I like him. I'm sure he'll do the company a lot of good." I pause. "As for my job, no way. I wouldn't want it back anyway."

***

Thanks to the suntan and the news about Emirates Energy, I feel like a million bucks on the morning drop-off. I've figured out that a huge pair of sunglasses hides a plethora of cosmetic tardiness, and my nails and hair are looking healthier than they have in a very long time. Most importantly, I've had another email about freelance work.

 I don't go straight home, though, to start on the piece, as it's the Year Two swim gala, and now I'm not tied to the office I can do things like watch our little tadpoles swim. The demo is scheduled to start at eight fifteen, which means between drop-off and taking our positions around the edge of the pool, there are a few spare minutes to grab a quick Costa coffee. Of course, this takes longer than I'd expected, and so when I get to the pool, it's standing room only.

 The turquoise water is clear, the kids excited. It's hot, but in the shade it's pleasant. There are benches set out, and a clever cooling device – a sort-of sprinkler-fan – whips the air with puffs of cool mist that catch the light in a way that reminds me of the sun glinting off the sea on a glorious day. Birds wheel and chirp overhead. I stand next to Host Mum, who's already been for a jog round the school perimeter.

 "Really?" I exclaim, still tasting the buttery croissant I'd eaten at Costa.

 Across the water, sixty children sit cross-legged – all wearing green-and-white swimming uniforms and swim caps. And herein lies my problem. It's almost impossible to work out which one is Jacob. Even when they stand up in small groups, and dive in, the combination of dazzling sunshine and regulation plastic caps makes it difficult to distinguish between them. Once in the pool, the churning water, arm thrashing and splashing hardly helps.

There are some remarkable swimmers among school children in Dubai. Given that they swim so regularly, both at school and for fun, it wouldn't surprise me if the next Michael Phelps comes from the emirate. These six and seven-year-olds make it look easy, slicing through the water like fish, their arms thrashing away as though controlled by a metronome. The smooth strokes of the kids in swim squad are a pleasure to watch.

There's a lot of cheering and noise. The swim mums (and dads) are easy to spot. "*Go!*" "*Kick harder!*" I wasn't joking when I said there's Olympic potential. I'm quite sure some of the mums are multi-tasking – watching their little 'uns swim like silver fish jumping upstream while also keeping one eye on their smartphone for prospective endorsement deals.

But after an hour of watching endless races in which my son may or may not have been participating, my enthusiasm is beginning to wane and my feet hurt. Circles of perspiration have begun to form on the parents' clothes. I pity the men in suits. By now, the temperature must have hit the mid-90s. As enjoyable as it was, I'm relieved to slink off home before we all melt, having escaped the rumoured 'parents' race'.

Later, I find myself in trouble, though. "Mum!" cries Jacob at pick-up time. He has his indignant voice on and a sulky face he appears to be experimenting with. "You weren't watching. *You didn't see me win!* Mum! WHY WEREN'T YOU WATCHING?"

I'm queuing up to pay for the weekly groceries the next morning when another strange sensation flutters inside me. I picture Host Mum's Victoria Sponge and decide if she can do it, why can't I? I just need the ingredients. I duck back to the baking section and scan the shelves, grabbing what I think I need and a new packet of cupcake mix with blue icing and white chocolate sprinkles for Jacob.

After school, Jacob and I get busy. Once his cupcakes are in the oven, giving off a sweet, freshly baked smell, I start on the Victoria Sponge. I've chosen an American recipe, which seems to contain a hundred per cent more butter and sugar than the British recipes, and will surely be a hundred per cent more scrumptious. It just needs adapting into a proper Victoria Sponge cake.

The first step is to cream the butter and sugar for seven whole minutes, until its light, pale and fluffy. Thirty seconds in, my mixer breaks. It proves impossible to fix and frustration seizes me. I try a hand-operated mixer I didn't even know I had, and quickly discover that even if I did have the right technique, it would be hard to operate it effectively for seven long minutes. *Damn, this really isn't as easy as I thought.*

I splash some wine into a glass and take an enormous gulp.

I'm about to take another sip when the idea to borrow a mixer from next-door pops into my head (I'm nothing if not resourceful). I rush over there, in my apron with cake dough smeared all over the front, and my amazed neighbour saves the day, her eyes too big for her lids at my domestic transformation.

The result, an hour-and-a-half later, looks nothing like Host Mum's cake. My distressed Victoria Sponge is lopsided, and the jam's all oozing out, but John and Jacob don't mind. They hungrily devour two slices as I tidy up the biggest mess I've ever seen in the kitchen.

Sitting down at my laptop after finishing the washing up, I bring up my Hotmail. I've misplaced my phones somewhere and haven't checked my email all afternoon. I'm sipping cool wine and feeling quite accomplished, if not for how the cake looked then for how happy it made my perpetually peckish family. Satisfaction mingles with the Australian red to create a warm glow inside me, and I decide I'll do half an hour's research into my freelance piece.

I have to click off Hotmail when I see the message, as if it's a venomous snake threatening to bite me. I let out a small sigh. Then, a few moments later, I go back to Malcolm's email and read it again, my hand hovering over the mouse.

"Julie, I've been trying to call you all afternoon. You'll have heard the news about Emirates Energy, I presume. Please respond ASAP. Could you come to the office in the morning? I have an offer for you. We really need you back in the fold."

***

The elevator takes me to the twentieth floor, stopping at least five times on the way up. I haven't missed this journey to the top of the tower at all. The box-like space is cramped and crowded, and I stand with my back pressed against the wall, watching Elevision to pass the time. I take small, shallow breaths to avoid choking on the strong scent of body odour permeating the stale air.

The doors slide open and I use my keycard to enter the reception. I'd half-expected it to not work, but the glass door releases and I walk inside. A girl I haven't seen before is sitting behind the desk.

"Hello, I'm here to see Malcolm," I say. "Julie Wainscote."

"Yes, he's expecting you," she replies, picking up a phone. "I'll see if he's ready." She points to two black leather chairs with a sorry-looking pot plant stationed between them on a small table. "Do take a seat."

I've sailed through this space so many times, without paying any attention to where people wait – in fact, I probably barely noticed the visitors patiently waiting. A courier is buzzed in and also told to sit, and I make a point to smile at him. I look at the plant as if seeing it for the first time – its leaves are lanky and pale, wilting from the lack of light.

"Julie, how are you?"

I look round and see Debbie. Her eyes look at little too wide awake. She must have had Botox again. She was always on at me to try it.

"Good," I say, smiling. "And you?"

"I'm fine. Missing you around here." She lowers her voice. "It's not the same without you. You look really well, by the way. You're positively glowing!"

"Gardening leave seems to suit me."

"You're so … brown!" She raises her own toned, bare arm and holds it against mine to compare tans, then drops it back to her side, bracelets jangling. "Come, Malcolm really wants to talk to you."

I hurry to his office, past the square edges, cubicles and rows of computers, saying a few quick hellos but not wanting to see too many colleagues. As the door clicks shut, I feel the familiar flood of adrenaline that always used to hit me before important meetings. It's almost a relief to discover my ambition and drive are intact.

We sit, very awkwardly at first as Debbie comes back with drinks and Malcolm starts on what turns out to be a long explanation about why he had to ask me to leave – and why he now wants me back.

His expression grows rueful.

I arrange my feet and knees in a straight line and lock eyes with him. I want to see him squirm even more before I say anything. It succeeds and he apologises again.

"Of course, this offer comes with a significant salary increase," he says. "At least 8,000dhs a month more – which is extremely competitive in today's marketplace."

I notice that his lips are moving, but the creases around his eyes are completely still. His eyes are vacant.

"This is a much higher offer than any other publisher in the Middle East could stretch to."

"Thank you," I say. "But no thank you. I really can't accept unfortunately."

"Do you have another job offer? We can match it."

I shake my head.

"Will you think about it?"

I say I will, more to get out of the office than anything else, and beat a hasty retreat before he becomes even more persuasive.

That evening, I discuss it with John. Malcolm has sent an email detailing the terms of a renewed contract, and instead of deleting it, I printed it out. I hold it in my hand. A glass of wine in my other hand. Jacob is in bed. I should be feeling happy, but I'm not. I'm confused. I'm still reeling from seeing our Dewa bill – 8,000dhs for electricity and water, and we don't even have a big garden; I just water my pots. I'm thinking about all sorts of things, school fees, college bills, retirement, the holidays we've grown accustomed to taking in far-flung parts of the world.

"What would you think if I went back?" I say in a small, unsure voice.

John shrugs. "It's up to you love. I'll support you either way. Wouldn't you prefer to carry on with the freelance work?"

"I don't know. No one's actually paid me so far. That side of it can be like getting blood out of a stone."

"Yes, but they'll pay eventually. They have to in Dubai – or they'll go to jail."

"True." I notice John is picking fluff off the arm of the chair. "But if I accept, imagine how much money we could save," I say. "We might even be able to afford that holiday home in France.

"It's not all about the money, though, is it?"

"I could just do it for a few more years. I do … I do miss it," I finally admit.

"If it's what you want … " His voice trails off then comes back stronger. "Look. Jules. Yes, the money would be good. It might be tax-free in this country, but the cost of living is so high here. We both know that."

I nod.

"We essentially pay to breathe," he continues. "God knows how our grocery bill is so high, when we've only bought bread and fish fingers." A deep perplexed line appears between his eyes as if Jacob had drawn it there with a biro. "But I honestly just want you to be happy. We can live on one salary – with a few adjustments."

I silently purse my lips. I feel as though I've been reeled in like a fish caught on a hook. "I do want to go back," I say. "It'll be different this time. I won't let it take-over my life – our lives – so much. You and Jacob, you're my priority. It's been wonderful having these past few weeks at home, but I feel ready … I want to give it another go. And we'll save, save, save like crazy, then I'll step back again once we've got our nest egg."

***

I decide to go to the meeting about the Winter Festival, despite knowing I'll have to backtrack on my involvement. I'm hoping they can find me a smaller role I can combine with work. The meeting is at Drama Mum's house, and when I arrive there are already a couple of women drinking coffee on the sofa. Their tanned legs end in exfoliated feet with painted toenails in flashy colours; there's a low teak-wood coffee table in front of them, laden with napkins and a large wooden board piled with all kinds of cheese, crackers, dried apricots and nuts.

The morning's agenda is dominated by talk about sponsorship and organising camel rides for the festival. When the conversation turns to our children and teachers, and the clinking of plates and cups peters out, I announce my change of circumstances. The women pretend to be pleased for me.

Drama Mum looks surprised, her furrowed brow suggesting concern. A second passes, then she regains her composure and smiles. I promise to find out if my company is willing to be a sponsor. It seems the least I can do.

Standing in the hallway on the way out, Drama Mum gently takes my arm. "Are you sure about going back?" she asks. "It really did sound like you were at your wit's end with the job."

I raise one shoulder in the tiniest of shrugs. "They made me an offer I couldn't refuse."

"Your freelance work was going really well, wasn't it?"

"It was building up nicely, yes. But this job won't be forever," I say, more to convince myself than my new friend. "I really hope we'll still be able to get together."

"Me too," says Drama Mum, gathering me into a hug and wishing me good luck.

That evening I'm making dinner when Malcolm calls to ask if I can attend to some important emails urgently. "It can't wait?" I ask. "I'll be in tomorrow."

"Really needs to be done tonight. Sorry." I can hear the sales director's voice in the background and realise they're still in the office. I'm not sure why I'm surprised. They work late most nights. "Gotta go," he says, hanging up, and I'm left listening to a lifeless line.

John raises his eyebrows. "I don't want to say I told you so, love."

I take care of the emails after dinner and put Jacob to bed. He's subdued and doesn't go down easily. He knows he's back on the school bus in the morning, and mummy won't be there when he gets home. I thought he'd taken it quite well, but about an hour after he falls asleep, I realise I was wrong.

A cry in the dark floats down the stairs. It starts out small then grows in intensity. The howl is high pitched and raw, and sounds wrong in Jacob's childish voice. I race upstairs.

The nightlight is on in his bedroom, and Jacob is sitting up in bed, glassy-eyed. It's hard to tell if he's asleep or awake. "It's okay," I whisper, and he starts to sob louder, his shoulders trembling. I pull him into my arms.

"What's the matter?" I ask gently, laying my hand against his forehead in case he's getting sick. He's hot from crying, but there's no fever. "Just a night terror," I murmur, stroking his hair. His eyes flutter shut.

He sleeps soundly for the rest of the night, but I don't. I toss and turn. In the end, I go to the spare room, as I'm disturbing John. By morning, I feel like a shell of my former self. I can move, talk and make breakfast, but I've switched onto automatic again. I don't feel particularly alive, yet I'm rushing around like a whirling dervish. I attempt to eat some toast, but it splinters in my mouth and sticks in my throat. I wave Jacob off on the school bus like a marionette, and feel bereft once he's gone. I'm beginning to think I've made a huge mistake.

The drive to work passes in much the same way. I'm functioning but not feeling anything other than dread and a deep sense of unease. I can steer, navigate traffic and brake, but a numbness has settled over me. I get the feeling again that I'm going to my execution.

As I near the office tower and join a traffic jam at the lights, I look up at the grey concrete-and-glass exterior; the windows seem ominous, staring back at me like empty eyes. There's no colour; just twenty-four storeys ascending blandly into the sky.

A horn blasts behind me.

I snap right back into the driver's seat. The light had turned green and I was a few milliseconds slow in moving off. I can see the driver in my rear mirror and every muscle in his face looks clenched.

At the car park, the barrier stays firmly down and more hoots ring out. My electronic opener must have died.

I'm not meant to be here. The corporate world isn't mine anymore.

I suddenly know what to do, with such clarity it's as though a blinding flash has gone off in my mind. I don't want to be a shadowy figure in Jacob's life; a ghost about to happen. I don't want to come home so tired that it's impossible to focus on anything other than hitting the sheets as quickly as possible. I can't spend my life spread so thinly across too many things. I don't want to miss out anymore. I want to perfect my Victoria Sponge, write freelance features, maybe even a book.

I'd rather be class mum, even if it means quietly going mad organising coffee mornings, liaising between home and school, collecting money and finding volunteers for school trips, swimming, and most recently for Drama Mum, the talent show.

The parking attendant raises the barrier, and I drive in. I do one lap round, then drive right out again and go straight home.

THE END

Acknowledgements

Thank you to every single person who has read my blog (dubaiunveiled.com) over the years, especially to those who have commented, given me encouraging feedback and generally cheered me on in my ramblings. The blog would have petered out long ago if it wasn't for you! Beginning its life as a travel diary, it's now the length of at least three novels and documents all the wonderful quirks (warts and all) of expat life here in the glorious city of Dubai. Writing a blog has also been a lot cheaper than therapy, and has put me in contact with so many smart, open-minded people all over the world. Thank you to all of you.

Do stop by my corner of the internet, if you haven't already. I promise you'll leave feeling entertained. And I promise all the characters in this book are fictitious with any resemblance to real people in Dubai (mostly) coincidental.

I can't thank my contributors – Inessa, Lucy and Lynn – enough for letting me use their work; their posts and stories are my favourites by far. I also want to thank my writing group (Inessa Jackson again, Michelle Stephens, Kate Witton, Claire Nice, Nicolette Kaponis and Keryn Donnelly) – one of these days I'll make it to Australia for an IRL (in real life) workshop. This book would never have seen the light of day if it wasn't for you guys and your amazing support.

Finally, a very special thank you to my family, my dad for passing on his love of books, my mum for spotting all my spelling and grammar mistakes, my husband for believing in me and putting up with me tapping away at all hours, and my boys for all the joy and love they bring me every day (I promise I'll stop writing about you when you become teenagers!)

To find out more about my fiction, please visit my website and blog, Circles in the Sand (dubaiunveiled.com). Follow me on Twitter (@circlesDubai); Instagram (@circlesinthesandblog); or Facebook (www.facebook.com/MarianneMakdisi.author)